Wicca Teachings

An Introduction and Practical Guide

Tony Bell

LAPWING
BOOKS

To Tony Anderson, who has stood by me through everything
and gives me inspiration every day

To Deborah Buchan, who was a guiding light to me

To Linda O' Connell, a proper Salem Witch who has helped me so much
through the years

And to Richard W Hardwick, a very talented writer and publisher who has
made this book and my dream possible

Lapwing Books
31 Southward
Seaton Sluice
Northumberland NE26 4DQ

A catalogue reference for this book is available from the British Library.

ISBN 978-0-9569555-2-4

Back cover artwork by Zoe Kralj and Victorija Poposka

Interior artwork by Fanni Károly

Printed by CreateSpace, An Amazon.com Company

Available on Kindle and other devices

Hear now the words of the witches
The secrets we hid in the night
When dark was our destiny's pathway
That now we bring forth into light

The Witches' Creed, Doreen Valiente

Contents

Introduction

When I first decided to become Wiccan I started to read books on the subject and quickly learned there were many conflicting views and stories about Wicca. There were bulky academic books that were hard to understand or fluffy fun spell books. There were books about covens, books about solitary witches, books about the history of Wicca and books about magic or witchcraft. But there were no straight to the point books that told you how to live your life as a Wiccan and exactly what Wicca was and what Wiccans believed. I became frustrated and sought answers online, joining many Wicca websites and forums but I found people there very impatient and quite harsh to new Wiccans wanting to learn. There was a suggestion that those new to the belief were lazy for not doing their own research, which in turn often led to those in the know being reticent to help. As well as becoming more and more frustrated at the way people coming into Wicca were being treated, I also encountered a great number of sites promoting 'The Dark Arts', something which is definitely not Wicca. Others stated, as a matter of fact, that Wicca was a new religion created by Gerald Gardner; again not true.

Throughout the following years though, I learned all I could about Wicca. I found many excellent books and websites, made numerous Wiccan friends and talked to some very learned scholars on the subject - until I acquired a particularly defined view of all Wiccans and the beliefs they held.

I started my own facebook page, Wicca Teachings, dedicated to teaching Wicca to new and experienced Wiccans alike. It's a page where I gather all the knowledge I've learned over the years and simply share it with others. The response has been phenomenal; over two million views per day. just six months later. It's now a community where Wiccans from all over the world, new and old alike, make new friends and help each other out. But many Wiccans are as frustrated as I was years before. I received hundreds of messages every week stating they'd read all the books and drudged through the many sites and still they did not know what it was to be Wiccan. Eventually, I'd been asked so many times to write a book myself, that I did – and so here it is.

I was raised in a Christian family in the North-East of England. My grandmother was of a much stricter faith than the rest of the family; going to church three or four times every week. As a child, I would go with her most times. The rest of the family only went to church for weddings, christenings or funerals but I've always felt very spiritual. From a young age though, I started questioning the church and its teachings. Something never sat right with me. When I prayed to God I would end my prayer to God and Mother Nature, not realising at the time I was actually praying to a God and Goddess. As a teenager I moved away from Christianity and looked into different religions; Hinduism, Buddhism, Islam and Judaism amongst others. I came upon Wicca by accident, or so it seemed at the time. A friend knew I was spiritual, interested in witchcraft and believed myself to be psychic. She bought me a book on Tarot which I loved, and inside this book the author mentioned Wicca, so I took a book out of the library and it immediately hit me that this is what I was and had always been without even knowing it. I had always been deeply in tune with nature and the seasons. I knew there was a God - and a Goddess, and I believed very much in magic. It hit home with me and I have never looked back since.

I've since realised of course, that all those old religions such as Christianity, Judaism and Islam are actually steeped in a much more ancient Pagan history. And I now know that the roots of Pagan beliefs were taken and warped by these supposedly traditional religions that then cut entirely the root of the divine feminine and replaced it with male control and fear.

I do not tell you this to cause division and anger. I wish peace on everyone, of every faith. But we must realise that our religions run much deeper than we are taught. Our Pagan ancestry goes back to the beginning of time, and all religions lead back to the Gods and Goddesses of old. Once we stop shouting about the differences in our religions and start shouting about how we are the same it will bring peace. When people stop being lied to and truths are revealed we will unite as a common human consciousness.

Wicca can lead the way towards a more peaceful and loving world, into a return to nature, from whence we came and are all still part of. This book cuts out the unnecessary and tells you what you need to know. It tells you what Wicca is and what it is not. I teach Wicca in a very easy to learn way and I will show you what it means to be Wiccan and how to live your life day by day as a Wiccan. I will show you the tools to perform magic spells and potions on your own so you will never need to buy another spell book again. This is exactly the kind of book I needed when I first decided to become Wiccan. And if you're wondering about Wicca yourself, or different teachings and theories have led you to become confused, then I'm guessing this is exactly the book for you too.

Thank you for reading and Blessed Be.

"The religion of the future will be a cosmic religion. It should transcend a personal God and avoid dogmas and theology. Covering both the natural and the spiritual, it should be based on a religious sense arising from the experience of all things natural and spiritual as a meaningful unity."

Albert Einstein

What is Wicca?

You do not need an altar to be Wiccan. You do not need a cauldron, a broomstick or a wand. In fact, you do not need anything whatsoever to be Wiccan. These items do not have anything to do with the spiritual aspect of Wicca; they are simply material props that help us with our magical workings. You do not need to be a part of a coven and you do not need to be initiated into Wicca, even though many covens or groups follow that procedure. If you believe and hold the God and Goddess in your heart, if you are at one with nature and the elements and if you believe there is magic in everything, then you are Wiccan. It really is as simple as that.

It is true that some branches of Wicca insist upon initiation into a coven to learn their secrets; examples of these are Gardnerian Wicca, named after Gerald Gardner, and Alexandrian Wicca, named after Alexander Sanders. This is all fine if you wish to join one of the many Gardnerian or Alexandrian covens around the world, but in modern Wicca the majority of Wiccans don't belong to a coven and instead practice their Wiccan faith in their own way. Wicca has many different branches to its tree and it's up to you to choose what feels most right for you.

Wicca is a nature based religion, a peaceful and empowering religion with a proud history. We worship nature, the seasons, the elements and the universe. Our deities are ancient Gods and Goddesses that predate other religions by thousands of years. Most modern things in today's society were built and invented by Pagan civilizations, including architecture, roads, lavatories, the wheel, wine making, language, writing and even religion. In fact the concept that there is a God or Gods was also a Pagan notion. Wiccans today still live by numerous Pagan ideals such as using a calendar. Pagan civilizations invested a lot of their time sky watching and season watching and built their lives around the cycles they observed. It helped them survive and prosper. It helped them turn into us, a modern society that, with the help of newer and more oppressive religions, now believes humans are more important than the rest of mother earth. It's time to turn the clock back. Wiccans believe earlier people on earth had a closer relationship with the divine. We want to learn all we can from ancient civilizations and their peoples as well as their Gods and Goddesses.

Every day 'ordinary' people live by Pagan ways without even knowing it. Many people call themselves 'spiritual' but would not admit to being Pagan because of negative connotations fostered by an oppressive Church and an ignorant media looking for an easy stereotype or cutting cliché. And yet, look around and you will see Paganism everywhere. The days of the week are named after our Gods and Goddesses. The twelve months of the year are named after Pagan Gods too, and that's not all. The planets of our solar system are all named after Pagan Gods, as are many stars, galaxies and constellations.

Many holidays that modern religions observe were once Pagan, such as Christmas, which is Yule when the Sun is born in the Winter Solstice. These holidays predate Christianity by thousands of years. Easter used to be known as Ostara which was celebrated in Spring when the Sun had risen again after a long Winter. It is the time of the earth being fertile, which is why it is represented by rabbits and eggs - fertility symbols. Samhain (Halloween) became All Saints Day. When the Christians were trying to convert Pagans to Christianity they kept many of the holidays Pagans celebrated to ease them into being Christian, but they changed the name and meaning to represent Christianity instead. Pope Gregory understood that the Britons and Angles in these lands were steeped in a Pagan way of life and that conversion by force and the destruction of Pagan festivals and holidays would be foolhardy and only cause resentment. His letter to St Augustine, dated 12 July AD 594, tells him "not to destroy the pagan temples, but rather to replace the idols with the relics of saints; to sprinkle the old precincts with holy water and rededicate them, because people come more readily to the places where they have been accustomed to pray. At festivals the people shall be allowed to build their booths of green leaves and to slay their bulls."

Of course, this holistic, non-judgemental approach didn't continue; it was simply a way of enticing the people in a slow and careful way. Before long the Christian church was demanding the destruction of sacred groves and insisting the worship of trees and stones was in fact demonic. Next came the persecution of the wise or cunning women, those who understood the healing power of plants, yet were killed for being 'evil witches.'

Many rituals performed by other religions are steeped in Pagan history too. Catholics use incense to bless an altar before mass. This is a pagan custom of clearing energy from an altar and setting shields of protective energy before ritual. Candles are lit upon church altars to beckon the presence of Jesus. Again, this is a Pagan custom, going back thousands of years, honouring and calling upon the God and Goddess. Holidays are named after the Holy Days of Pagan descent. Weddings, funerals, baptisms and circumcisions all are of pagan origin, and so the list goes on.

There are many Pagan monuments too, such as the Washington Monument in Washington DC, an ancient Egyptian worship temple called an Obelisk, erected to worship the Sun Gods in ancient Egypt. There's another one in the centre of the Vatican City. The Statue of Liberty is a statue of the Roman Goddess Libertas, who is the Goddess of Liberty, Truth and Justice. There are Pagan monuments all over the world and there are still many being built to this day. See if you can find some near you; you might be surprised.

Contrary to popular belief, Wiccans are not evil or bad, and nor do we worship the devil or Satan. The devil is a Christian concept and so you must first be Christian to believe in him.

Wiccans do not believe in the devil; he was a fallen angel of the Christian God. And Wiccans do not worship any other evil or bad demons whatsoever. We understand that we all have dark and light inside us and we work on keeping the two in balance. We do not blame any outside source for bad behaviour; instead we blame ourselves if we do something wrong and we understand it will come back to us in a karmic way as is the laws of nature and the universe.

Throughout modern history, witches have been portrayed as evil, or as old hags or whores of the devil, mainly because of ignorance capitalised on and fuelled by religious dogma, media, books and fairy tales. In reality, witches were the wise elders of country villages, healers, midwives, philosophers and spell casters. If you had a problem you would go the Wicca or Witch as the name is now better known. Early Christian stance on this practice was to simply dismiss it all as superstition, but in the early medieval period the church recognised the power these women had and that their previous more passive stance had not been successful. And so consequently, they set out to destroy them. Throughout Europe and the European colonies of North America mass hysteria was created, alleging that witches were worshippers of the devil. Prosecutions peaked in the 16th and 17th centuries but also continued afterwards. In three centuries it's reckoned that between 40,000 and 100,000 people, mainly women, were killed, usually by drowning, torture, hanging or being burned alive at the stake. Thankfully, although negative stereotypes of paganism and witches continue today, we don't have to suffer such terrible consequences. In fact, nowadays the axis is turning, with many people realising there is a void in their life that can only be filled by the beauty and power of nature and spirituality.

Now is the time! Embrace the change and come back to the old ways. You don't have to give up everything that is modern. The internet and smartphones are wonderful tools that can help us connect with each other. All I ask is that you learn, understand and respect the beauty and power of nature and use it wisely and without harm.

Some consider Wicca to be a new age religion started in the 1950s by a man named Gerald Gardner. This is not true. Even though Gardner had a massive influence on Wicca and helped make the religion as well-known as it is today, he did not invent Wicca. The word Wicca comes from an ancient Old English word meaning Witch. Wicca and Witchcraft have been intertwined since ancient times and it is not a new age religion of the 20th century. If anything, Christianity, Judaism and Islam are new age religions as Paganism and Wicca outdate them by thousands of years.

Wiccan religion today is based on ancient witchcraft, but also lends ideas from many other ancient civilizations and cultures. To put it simply a Wiccan is a Witch who is also a Pagan. Not all witches are Pagans though; some go by their own rules, good or bad. Witches come from all walks of life and follow many different religions. A Wiccan is a certain type of witch that lives by the law of the land and in conjunction with nature, hence making them Pagan.

Some people can find all this a little confusing, so below is a brief description of the difference between a Pagan, a Witch and a Wiccan.

Paganism

Paganism is an umbrella term to mean a person who follows any nature-based religion. A pagan therefore, is someone who worships nature. They follow a set of religious guidelines drawn out by natural occurrences including the seasons and the phases of the moon and sun. Nature, it could be said, is a pagan's church in which to worship in. A pagan usually believes in both a God and a Goddess, with an emphasis on balance, much like nature itself. In several beliefs of Paganism there are numerous Gods and Goddesses that represent a planet, a celestial body or some other form of nature. Such religions that fall under this umbrella are Wicca, Shintoism, Asatru, Shamanism, Druidry and, to some, even Hinduism. Additionally, a pagan may be atheist or heathen and not have any Gods, but simply follow the laws of nature.

Witchcraft

Witchcraft is a craft, a skill that involves making things. A witch is someone who practices witchcraft by means of chants, incantations, spells, potions, herbalism, aromatherapy, stones, crystals and natural healing. Some witches use divination to see into the future, either through being psychic themselves or by using tools such as Tarot Cards, Rune Stones, Crystal Balls and Palmistry. A witch can follow many paths. They may not be religious at all and may not believe in any Gods. They may be Christian, in that they practice witchcraft but follow the Christian religion. Alternatively, they may practice or follow Black Magic or Voodoo. A witch can be many different things and sometimes they are simply just a witch.

Wicca

A Wiccan is someone who is pagan and also a witch that practices witchcraft as part of their religion. Wiccans follow the moon phases, performing different rituals and magic on certain times of the moon phases. In Wicca the moon is the Goddess and the sun is the God. In some branches of Wicca, such as Gardnerian, there is only one God and one Goddess (the moon and the sun) but many Wiccans, calling themselves Eclectic Wicca, believe in multiple Gods and Goddesses.

Wiccans use nature as part of their magical rituals and workings. For example, when the moon is waxing (coming into being full) a Wiccan will do spell work that brings things to them and will ask for positives to be brought into their lives. When the moon is waning (going away after a full moon) they will ask bad things to leave their lives and work to expel negativity. Full moons are called Esbats and much ritual and magical work is done on these nights. To a Wiccan a spell, chant or meditation is like a prayer. The sun, our God who seeds and fertilizes the earth, is celebrated on eight holidays we call Sabbats which fall throughout the year on seasonal changes to the earth. Wicca takes from many ancient pagan civilizations and cultures including Native Americans, ancient Rome, ancient Greece, ancient Egypt, Norse Vikings, Aztecs, Incas, Celts, Druids and Anglo-Saxons. It is said that not all Witches are Wiccan but all Wiccan are Witches.

Wicca is a non-restrictive religion that leaves you to choose your own path, and there are many different paths of Wicca so you must choose the one that feels right for you. We all have the same fundamental belief, but we choose to practice in different ways, similar to many faiths, including Christianity, with its Catholic, Presbyterian, Protestant, Amish and other branches.

Wicca encourages you to empower yourself, to stay positive and keep negativity at bay. We embrace our dark side as well as our light and seek to balance the two. Our actions are our own and are not blamed on an outside force such as evil, demons or the devil.

Wicca, unlike many new age religions such as Christianity, Islam and Judaism, does not follow the word of man or a monotheistic God; instead Wicca follows the divine and awesome power of nature; the stars, the sun and moon, the universe. Wicca follows stories of ancient Gods passed down from ancestors from the beginning of time.

In Wicca we do not have churches or buildings to pray in. We use nature as our church and our place to worship. Wicca does not ask for money to keep the religion alive, while the leaders get rich and live in palaces and castles and the worshippers live in poverty. Wicca does not ask anything from you. It does not ask us to ostracise or hate certain people, because of where they were born or because of their sexuality. Instead Wicca encourages people's individuality and asks that they find their own spiritual path. It goes against everything Wiccans stand for to judge others; we are all emotional and perceptive beings and should be allowed to be ourselves and live our lives free from pain or harassment.

Balance is essential within Wicca. Balance means to be free of drama and neurotic behaviour, to not allow your past or guilt take over your life, but also to not let the future and what is still to come take over your life either. Live in the present and take each thing as it comes. We learn from our past and move on, we prepare in the here and now to create our own future. We accept our light and our dark, our feminine and our masculine as one cannot be without the other.

"I have been told by witches in England: 'Write and tell people we are not perverts. We are decent people, we only want to be left alone, but there are certain secrets that you mustn't give away.' So after some arguments as to exactly what I must not reveal, I am permitted to tell much that has never before been made public concerning their beliefs, their rituals and their reasons for what they do; also to emphasize that neither their present beliefs, rituals nor practices are harmful."

Gerald Gardner

Wicca Paths and Traditions

There are, admittedly, purists within Wicca who insist certain things must be done in the traditional way; otherwise it must be wrong. Sadly all religions have purists who insist theirs is the right way and anywhere or anything else is heading down the wrong path. But Wicca has many different paths and traditions and there is no right or wrong way to be Wiccan. Wicca is a living religion that is ever growing and evolving, although it must be noted that all paths do follow the eight Sabbats and twelve Esbats. Apart from that you are free to choose and so, to help you, here's a brief description of different Wiccan Paths you may want to consider following.

Old Wicca

Wicca is an old English (Anglo Saxon) word meaning witch. If you were a witch in England and most of Europe you would have been called a Wicca (male) or Wicce (female). The word also means 'Wise' or 'Wise One', which is appropriate given Wicca were the village healers, sages and wise people, called upon for many things including midwifery, fortune telling and convening with the Gods. In nearly all ancient cultures and civilizations there were wise people who would treat the sick, foretell future events, bless births and marriages. People who follow the old path are Eclectic Wicca and incorporate many Gods and Goddesses into the religion. They are mostly solitary witches who do not belong to a group or coven and learn through reading old accounts and books of the wise women, men and sages from ancient scriptures and records.

Gardnerian Wicca

Gardnerian Wicca was derived from a man named Gerald Gardner who used the old English name for Witch (Wicca) and turned it into a coven based religion. Gardner was taught about magic and witchcraft in 1938 when he joined a group called The Rosicrucian Order based on Freemasonry. The people in this coven called themselves Wica (with one 'c'). Gardner disagreed with many of the groups beliefs though and left disenchanted. In 1939 he was initiated into a Coven called New Forest in England, which was said to be a very old world coven with traditions passed down from many generations of Witches.

Around 1946 Gardner left the New Forest Coven and created The Bricklewood Coven. He taught people in his own unique way, taking on board steps and insights he'd learned from other groups. The Wicca he taught at Bricklewood went up in degrees, much like Freemasonry which Gardner was very interested in. Many of his witches reached the highest degree and became High Priestesses and Priests and went out and created their own Covens under Gardner's teachings, henceforth becoming known as Gardnerian Wiccans. Gardner was highly influenced by Alistair Crowley, a famous witch and social critic, and he also worked very closely with a woman called Margaret Murray to write 'Witchcraft Today,' published in 1954. Gardner felt Wicca was fragmented and wanted to draw all his experience and knowledge together to create a universal coven known today as Gardnerian Wicca. You must be initiated into a Gardnerian coven by the High Priest or Priestess and you must sign an oath to keep the coven's secrets when joining.

Alexandrian Wicca

Alexandrian Wicca, introduced by Alexander Sanders in the 1960s, is based heavily on the teachings of Gardnerian Wicca which Alexander Sanders (known as the Witch King in his circles) mentions in many of his books. Alexandrian Wicca is based on Gender polarity and all rituals are carried out with a High Priest and Priestess. While Gardnerian is strictly ritualistic and only believes in one God and one Goddess, with a High Priestess leading all rituals, Alexandrian Wicca lets you believe in whichever Gods and Goddesses you like. A saying in Alexandrian Wicca is, "If it works, use it." Alexander Sanders and his wife Maxine Sanders were both trained in the Gardnerian tradition, becoming a High Priest and Priestess, but they wanted to move away from it and make changes as they felt Gardnerian was too controlled and forced. Alexandrian Wicca adds aspects of the Hermetic Qabalah to the teachings. Alexandrian Covens meet on the New Moon, the Full Moon and on the eight Sabbats. Like Gardnerian Wicca, you must sign a secret oath when joining an Alexandrian Coven and you must first be initiated by the High Priest and Priestess.

Seax Wicca

Seax Wicca is a tradition founded by Raymond Buckland in 1973 and is detailed in his book 'The Tree - The Complete Book of Saxon Witchcraft.' This path follows the practice of the Anglo Saxon traditions, including Germanic Gods and Goddesses such as Woden and Freya. Raymond Buckley was a Gardnerian before founding Seax so numerous Gardnerian traditions are used in his book and within coven meetings. Buckley left the Gardnerian tradition as he wanted to create a coven where only the Anglo Saxon Gods and their traditions were used as a base for coven meetings. Unlike Gardnerian and Alexandrian Wicca you do not need to sign a secret oath to join a Seax Coven; in fact they are very open and welcoming to anyone interested in the tradition.

Dianic Wicca

Dianic Wicca is a feminist form of Wicca that is only for women, with its followers worshipping the Roman virgin hunter Goddess Diana. Founded by Zsuzsanna Budapest in the 1970s, this path follows the traditions of Gardnerian or Alexandrian Wicca. It has covens but they do not allow males and do all their ritual workings with only the High Priestess. Diana the Goddess is worshipped as all powerful and the source of all living things.

Hereditary Wicca

Hereditary Wicca pertains to those born into a Wiccan family and brought up within the Wicca tradition. This can come from any form of Wicca in which the family follow. If the family are involved in a coven then often the child will be given a choice around the time of their teenage years, where they can choose to join the coven or follow their own spiritual path.

Eclectic Wicca

About 70% of Wiccans are Eclectic, meaning they do not follow any specific Wicca tradition but instead choose the Gods and Goddesses they wish to worship, whether they be Norse, Egyptian, Roman, Greek or any other. Alternatively, they may worship them all believing they are all the same Gods and Goddesses but have been known by different names within different civilizations. Eclectic Wiccans are usually solitary in their practice of Wicca, celebrating Esbats and Sabbats at their own altar at home. However, there are many covens and groups for Eclectic Wiccans, where they choose their own way of convening meetings.

Solitary Wicca

Solitary Wicca is the fastest growing form of Wicca. As the name suggests, a solitary Wiccan does not belong to any coven or group. They may follow the one God and Goddess or they may follow all of the Gods and Goddesses. Solitary Wiccans celebrate Esbats and Sabbats and have their own altars at home for worship. They are mostly Eclectic Wicca that shun away from covens and specific traditions, preferring instead to make their own journeys and discoveries and follow their own spiritual path.

Faery Wicca

Faery Wiccans place emphasis on Faery lore or the Fae as they are known. These aren't the cartoon type of Faery such as Tinkerbell but sprites who keep everything balanced and moving in nature. The Faery has an extensive history in Britain, Ireland and the rest of Europe - and in lands whose natural beauty is still largely unspoiled, belief in faeries, sprites and elves remains strong. Faery Wiccans claim their beliefs originate from the early Celtic traditions of Tuatha De Danann.

Draconic Wicca

Draconic Wicca places emphasis on Dragons and Dragon lore. Dragons and their lore are ancient and have been worshipped, feared and talked about in almost every ancient culture in history. Artwork and cave drawings of such creatures have been found that bear striking resemblances to each other, and yet originate from cultures that had never connected with each other. Dragons are invoked during magical workings and are ruled over by the Sun God and the Moon Goddess. Each element has a dragon named after it, such as the Fire Dragon which is called upon for strength. Draconic Wicca is not very well known but has been growing steadily for a number of years. It is mostly found in Asian countries, but it is also growing in America and Europe.

"Dwell on her graciousness, dwell on her smiling,
Do not forget what flowers
The great boar trampled down in ivy time.
Her brow was creamy as the crested wave,
Her sea-blue eyes were wild
But nothing promised that is not performed."

Robert Graves - To Juan at the Winter Solstice

Gods & Goddesses

There are many Gods and Goddesses within Wicca; it just depends on which path of Wicca you have chosen to follow. And there are many different branches to the Wiccan tree, as there are in other religions.

Some Wiccans have the Roman Gods and Goddesses as their deities, some the Greek Gods and Goddesses and others the Egyptian Gods and Goddesses. Some worship Norse Gods and Goddesses, whilst others follow the Celtic tradition. The majority of Wiccans are Eclectic though; believing all ancient Gods and Goddesses are one and the same but with different names from different civilizations.

In Gardnerian teaching there is only one God and one Goddess, the God of the Sun and the Moon Goddess. This God is horned and is the God of the wild hunt and the keeper of everything wild, including animals, forests, woods, plants and trees. Usually named Cernunnos, he is part human and part stag with the antlers of a buck. In different traditions he may be called Pan who is part human and part goat with the horns of a ram. The Goddess is a triple Goddess; maiden, mother and crone. She gave birth to all things including the God who is her consort and helps sustain life on earth. In spring the triple Goddess is the maiden, young and fertile. In summer and early autumn she is the mother and in late autumn and winter she changes to the crone. Her cycle begins again at the turning of the wheel in spring, when she reverts to maiden once more.

You should choose what feels right to you. If you have more of an affinity towards Egyptian Gods and Goddesses that is fine, but if you feel closer to the deities of ancient Greece then that is fine too. The Gods and Goddesses you choose to follow are up to you. When you have chosen those you feel closest to, learn all you can about them. There are many books written on the ancient Pagan Gods and Goddesses and there are numerous excellent websites too.

The Gods and Goddesses may be worshipped and/or asked to help in your spell workings or seasonal rituals. If you were to do a fertility spell then you would call upon the fertility Goddess of your particular path or choosing. If you were doing a love spell then you would chose a God or Goddess of love to help you depending upon the pantheon you have chosen.

We make offerings to Gods and Goddesses to show our love and gratitude to them. They give us so much we like to give a little back to them, and this is especially important when we ask for anything during spell work. Remember everything is about balance; if you are bestowed with a gift after you have asked for it in spell work you should give something back to keep the balance. The offerings are something to honour the God you chose to work with whilst doing the spell work; for example, if it was the Goddess Persephone, the Greek Goddess of Spring, then we would give her flowers. We don't only offer gifts to the Gods if they help us though; we also give them gifts on our altars on special days such as a Sabbat or an Esbat as an offering of gratitude.

Wiccans have a very close relationship with the Gods. They are not some almighty powerful entity in the sky that will smite you if they are not happy with you. They are more like our allies, our friends. The Gods and Goddesses created humans and love us, and they want us to succeed and be happy, but they also like to be worshipped and acknowledged as it gives them strength. They have flaws just like we do; they did make us in their own image after all. They can be tricksters or generous, jealous or loving, and they can look favourably on you or at times ignore you. Our Gods and Goddesses are ancient and have been looking down over humanity since the beginning of time. Respect them, make a relationship with them, know them and love them. We honour the Gods with our actions. In everything we do we honour a certain God. If you do something brave or help someone you are honouring the Norse God Odin. If you do something artistic or poetic you are honouring the Greek God Apollo.

In magic we call upon the Gods and the Goddesses to help us with spell work and rituals. Below is a list of the Gods and Goddesses most associated with Wicca. I cannot write a full list of every God and Goddess in every pantheon as there are hundreds. Nor can I write a full list of every power of the Gods I've selected below because some have so many powers it's impossible to cover them all. Below are listed the Greek, Roman, Egyptian, Norse and Celtic Gods and Goddesses with a brief introduction only. These will give you a taste of each pantheon and help you choose which may feel right for you. But you should certainly research your chosen pantheon more fully.

Greek & Roman Gods and Goddesses

Most of the Greek Gods were also worshipped in Ancient Rome. Even though the names were changed they are ultimately the same Gods. Below I usually refer to Greek Gods for the sake of brevity, rather than any personal preference. If both names are mentioned then it is the Greek name that is mentioned first.

In the beginning, there was only chaos and nothing - but out of this nothingness came light. Gaia, the earth, Erebus, the underworld, and Night emerged from the mixing of chaos and light, and Gaia gave birth to Uranus, the heavens, who then became her mate, and Oceanus, the oceans. Gaia and Uranus together produced twelve Titans, three Cyclopes, and three hundred-handed giants, or Hecatoncheires, but Uranus feared his children as a threat to his throne, and bade Gaia take them back into her womb.

Gaia loved her children however, and hated Uranus' tyranny. She supplied her youngest child, Cronus, with a sickle, and told him to kill his father with it. He cut off Uranus' genitals, and these fell into the sea and from them were created Aphrodite, the Goddess of Love, and the Fates, the Giants, and the Meliai nymphs. Cronus succeeded Uranus on the throne and married his sister Rhea. He freed the Titans and shared his kingdom among them, but imprisoned the Cyclopes and the Hecatoncheires in Tartarus, a fiery pit much like Hell.

Cronus

Cronus was the leader and the youngest of the first generation of Titans, divine descendants of Gaia, the earth, and Uranus, the sky. He overthrew his father and ruled during the mythological Golden Age, until he was overthrown by his own son, Zeus and imprisoned in Tartarus. The Greeks considered him a cruel and tempestuous force of chaos and disorder, but the Romans believed him to be a more positive God.

Rhea / Cybele

In early traditions, Rhea is known as the Mother of Gods and therefore is strongly associated with Gaia, the earth. She gave birth to six children, but their father Cronus ate the first five. And so she hid the sixth, Zeus, in a cave in Crete. Zeus later forced his father to disgorge his siblings, and so back out came Hestia, Hades, Demeter, Poseidon and Hera. Rhea is often associated with the Roman Goddess Cybele.

Zeus / Jupiter

Zeus is the King of Gods, the head God of Mount Olympus. He has been weakened over the centuries as his power comes from being worshipped and with the introduction of many other religions he is not worshipped as much these days. Zeus is God of the Skies too. He sees to it that the good are rewarded and the bad punished.

Hera / Juno

Hera is the Goddess of the Sky, mostly the sky at night. She is also Goddess of Marriage, which includes revenge on people cheating in relationships. As the wife of Zeus she loved him very much, but Zeus had many affairs and his mistresses paid a heavy price at the hands of Goddess Hera, especially Leto, Semele and Alkmene, whom she played out a series of nasty revenges on.

Poseidon / Neptune

Poseidon, the brother of Zeus, is the God of Seas and Oceans. Later named Neptune by the Romans he had many lovers of both sexes. Poseidon created islands and offered calm seas, though his anger could cause earthquakes, drownings and shipwrecks. Not surprisingly, sailors prayed to him for a safe voyage.

Hades / Pluto

Hades is the Brother of Poseidon and Zeus. God of the Underworld, he drew lots with his brothers to decide on the parts of the earth they would rule over. Present at funerals to take the dead to the underworld, he abducted and married Zeus's daughter Persephone. Hades is also a God of Wealth because of the rich nutrients in the soil and the mines in which precious metals and diamonds are found.

Apollo

Apollo, son of the great God Zeus, is God of the Sun, and of Music, Art and Poetry. He is also God of Light, Truth and Healing. The rays of the Sun were Apollo's arrows, fired at humanity to provide inspiration, life and healing. He was named Apollo by both Greek and Romans.

Artemis / Diana

Artemis and Diana are Goddesses of the Hunt and are often depicted with a bow and arrow. It is said the crescent moon is their bow. Artemis, the twin sister of Apollo and a Moon Goddess, was later worshipped in ancient Rome as Diana. Artemis is also the Goddess of Childbirth and is said to assist women in labour. Diana and Artemis are fiercely independent. Both are virgins and will give their love to no man or God. Artemis, a skilful hunter, killed Orion when he tried to make advances towards her. She also killed Adonis for spreading word he was a better hunter than her.

Athena / Minerva

Athena is the Goddess of Wisdom, Mathematics, Science and Law and Justice, as well as many other things. She did not have a mother but was born straight from Zeus's brain. One of the most powerful of all Greek Gods and Goddesses, she competed with Poseidon to become Patron of Athens, the capital city of one of the greatest civilisations ever, and we can tell by the name of the city that she won. She is also the patron Goddess of teachers, intellect and clarity.

Aphrodite / Venus

Aphrodite is the Goddess of Love, the Goddess of Beauty, Pleasure and Procreation. She was born from the foam of the sea, is eternally young and beautiful, with charms that make her irresistible to anyone. She had affairs with many different Gods, including Ares and Adonis. Her son is Eros / Cupid, the God of Love.

Ares / Mars

Ares is the Greek God of War, the God of Courage and Fearlessness. If you need to call upon strength then call upon Ares; he loved fighting so much he was often said to have come down from the sky and joined in great battles, sending many men to Hades, which Hades was grateful for.

Hermes / Mercury

Hermes, son of Zeus, guides the dead to the underworld but is also messenger of the Gods, journeying from one God to the next at lightning speed. As he is a trickster and very cunning he is also the God of Thieves, whilst later he became the God of Shepherds.

Pan / Faunus

Pan, half goat and half man, burgeoning with sexuality and often depicted with an erect penis, is the God of the Wild, and of Forests and Shepherds. Likened to the Celtic God Cernunnos, he can also be seen playing a flute and is a God of Fertility.

Hestia / Vesta

Hestia is the sister of Zeus and Goddess of the Home and Family. She is known as the virgin Goddess, for when both Apollo and Poseidon asked for her hand in marriage she refused and told Zeus she wanted to remain a virgin for eternity so she could look after all families on earth.

Demeter / Ceres

Demeter is the Goddess of Agriculture and Farming. Sister of Zeus and daughter of Cronus and Rhea, she keeps the land fertile. Her daughter Persephone was abducted by Hades and forced to marry him. Helped by Artemis, Demeter searched everywhere for Persephone, eventually being told by the Sun God Apollo that her daughter had been abducted by Hades with Zeus's permission. As revenge she stopped all crops and flowers from growing. The land became barren. God's creations were slowly being destroyed. Zeus had little option but to grant permission for Persephone to be freed from the underworld. And yet, even though Persephone had been forced to marry Hades she had grown to love him too. She was granted freedom from the underworld because it was the only way to save the earth. A compromise was subsequently agreed, with her spending half the year on earth and half in the underworld.

Dionysus / Bacchus

Dionysus is the son of Zeus and Selene, the only mortal to have been made a God after Zeus had an affair with her. Selene knew Zeus was a God but she didn't know which one as it was simply his divine presence she loved. Hera, Zeus's wife, found out, disguised herself and went to see Selene. She told Selene that she needed to see the God she was in love with and only then could make her a Goddess. Zeus agreed to this and showed himself after they made love, but Selene was burnt to a crisp by the light of him. Zeus stitched Dionysus to his thigh and took him to the heavens where he was born, and because he was born of Zeus he became a God. Granted the title and power of God of Wine and of the Grape Harvest, Dionysus, perhaps understandably given the story surrounding his birth, is an unpredictable God. He can bring joy and ecstasy but can also be full of rage and violence.

Persephone / Proserpina

Persephone is the Goddess of Spring and Flowers and also of the Underworld. Homer describes her as the formidable, venerable majestic Queen of the Underworld, who carries into effect the curses of men upon the souls of the dead. One day, while out tending flowers, she was abducted by Hades, taken to the underworld and forced to marry him. Having fallen in love with him, she agreed to spend half her time on earth, because it was the only way her mother Demeter would allow crops and flowers to grow once more.

Aradia

Although strictly not a Roman Goddess, Aradia should be mentioned as she was said to be the daughter of the Roman Goddess Diana, and was sent down to earth as a messiah to set slaves free and teach witchcraft. When she had taught all she could she ascended back up into the heavens. To many witches Aradia is the divine Goddess of Witchcraft, as is her mother Diana. "Go to earth below / To be a teacher unto women and men / Who fain would study witchcraft," said Diana to her messiah daughter Aradia, according to 'The Gospel of the Witches' by Charles Leland, a text translated from the 14th century. Aradia then said unto the Coven, "Ye shall all be freed from slavery / And so ye shall be free in everything."

Egyptian Gods and Goddesses

Egyptians believed that at the beginning of time there was only blackness and chaos. The first God was Atum-Ra who sneezed and gave birth to Shu, the God of Water, and Tefnut, Goddess of the Air. Tefnut and Shu bore children, Nut the Goddess of Sky and Geb, God of the Earth. Shu and Tefnut went walking one day and became lost. Fearing something awful had happened to them Atum-Ra sent his all seeing eye to go and find them. His tears of joy then turned into humans.

Ra

Ra was the first God of the Sun, and of the Earth and Underworld. He sailed across the skies in his boat called Barque of Million Years. He died every day but left enough light to keep the Moon Goddess alive when he was in the underworld. He then sailed back to rise again every morning. Ra, who fought his worst enemy every day, a snake called Apep, was the greatest of all the Gods but could be cruel and unjust because when his power was so strong the sun was too hot for people to live and for crops to grow. At times rain dried before even reaching the ground. The loving Goddess Isis despaired seeing mankind suffer so she used magic to make a snake which she made from saliva from Ra and clay from the earth. She hid the snake where she knew Ra was going. When the snake bit Ra he screamed in agony which caused massive earthquakes on earth. Isis, as Goddess of Healing, told him she would be able to stop his pain but only if he spoke his real name to her, for Isis knew Ra's powers came from his secret name. Ra was in so much pain he had little option. And so, when he revealed his real name, Isis was able to claim the same powers that Ra had, making her an equal ruler. She then forced Ra to shine less brightly and eventually, because he was an aging God, he gave rule of the Sun to Horus and retired as a sky God to watch over mankind.

Isis

Isis, the first daughter of Geb and Nut, is the Goddess of Fertility, Mothers, Love and the Moon. She loves the people of earth and is said to walk among them to teach agriculture and crafting as well as showing women how to tame men enough to live with them. Isis became the most powerful Goddess by tricking Ra to stop him doing harm to mankind. She married her brother Osiris and made him God of all Earth. Osiris ruled with love and compassion, but the other brother Set was jealous and had Osiris killed so he could take his place as the lover of Isis and the Earth God. Isis, desperate with grief, ripped up her clothes and tore out her hair. She searched earth and eventually discovered Osiris's body hidden in a fragrant tree and carried it home. But Set was furious and ordered his brother's body chopped into fourteen segments and thrown in every direction, hoping they would be eaten by crocodiles. Isis then searched with the help of seven scorpions that protected her. She put Osiris's body back together as she found each piece, though she couldn't find his penis so fashioned one from gold and wax. Then, helped by Anubis and inventing mummification and embalming, she brought Osiris back to life and conceived a child with him named Horus. Now that Osiris had given Isis a child she allowed him to descend into the underworld. Horus became God of the Sun and Isis once again became a Moon Goddess.

Horus

Horus, son of Isis and Osiris, is the God of the Sun and Sky. He is the God of Protection and Magic too, and was God of all Pharaohs of Egypt. He has the head of a falcon and the body of man. In revenge for his father's murder by his Uncle Set, Horus ascended to be the Sun God and attacked him. Set gauged out Horus's eye but his mother Isis gave him a magical replacement that could see evil at all times. Set knew he could not win this battle though, so the two came to a truce with Horus ruling over day and Set ruling at night. This gave us the term Sun Set. The Eye of Horus is a magical symbol that can protect you against ill-will and evil.

Hathor

Hathor is the Goddess of Joy, Love and Motherhood. She is the wife of Horus and Goddess of the Sun. Hathor was one of the most beloved Goddesses in Ancient Egypt and was said to be mother to the pharaohs.

Bast

Bast is the Goddess of Cats, which were held in very high regard in Ancient Egypt. She is depicted with the head of a cat or lioness and is a protection Goddess as well as holder of the Eye of Horus and a sworn protector of the Sun Gods. Because of her protection status her statues can be placed in areas of the household where you feel the need to be protected.

Anubis

Anubis, God of the Dead, helped Isis embalm and mummify Osiris and lead him into the underworld after he finally died. He has the head of a jackal and the body of man and lies in wait for you in the 'Hall of the Dead' where he weighs your heart against the Goddess Ma'at's feather. Ma'at is the Goddess of justice and if your heart is lighter than her feather then you will live forever in the afterlife. But if your heart weighs more than the feather, it is eaten by a demon called Ammit which has the head of a crocodile, the body of a lion and the bottom quarters of a hippopotamus. Thoth the God of Words and Wisdom records everything that happens here.

Ma'at

Ma'at is the Goddess of Honour, Justice, Truth and Wisdom. She is the wife of Thoth and together they help Anubis in the underworld. Ma'at's feather is an ostrich feather which is used to weigh your heart before you are allowed into the underworld.

Thoth

Thoth, the God of Wisdom, invented writing and the hieroglyphs. Depicted with the head of an Ibis bird, he is a recorder of knowledge, recording every star that is born and dies and every human that is born and dies. There is said to be a 'Book of Thoth', containing two spells. If you read the first spell aloud you will understand every animal on earth and control all life of the sea. If you read aloud the second spell you will have the power to bring people back from the dead.

Tawaret

Tawaret is the Goddess of Childbirth and protects women in labour. She is depicted with the head of a hippopotamus, arms and legs of a lion, the back and tail of a crocodile and the breast and stomach of a pregnant woman. People wear her as an amulet to protect them when pregnant and to protect their children from harm.

Norse Gods and Goddesses

In the beginning there was nothing but a dark void, much like in Egyptian and Greek creation theory. The first being was Ymir the Giant, the first of a race of Frost Giants. Ymir fathered a six-headed son who suckled on a cow (the cosmos) called Audumla that fed by licking rhinestone until it was eventually shaped to the form of a man. This man was called Buri and was the first of the Gods. Buri then gave birth to Bor who married a Giant called Bestla and they gave birth to Gods such as Odin, Vili and Ve.

The Norse Gods can be separated into two different groups; the Aesir who are the main Gods and are protectors and war-like, and the Vanir, lesser peace loving Gods.

The world in which the Norse Gods live is called Yggdrasil, a giant tree (the universe) that is split into nine worlds. The first level is Asgard, home of the Aesir Gods. The second level is Vanaheim, home of the Vanir Gods. The third level is Alfheim, home of elves. The home of humans is Midgard (Middle Earth), situated on the fourth level. Midgard is connected to Asgard by a rainbow bridge made from frost. The fifth Level is Jotunheim where the ice giants live. The sixth is Svartalfheim, home of the dark elves. The seventh is Nidavellir, home of the dwarfs, and the eighth is Niflheim, home of the dead. The final level, the ninth, is Muspelheim, and this is the home of fire giants and demons.

Odin

Odin, or Woden as he is sometimes called in Anglo Saxon, is the king of all Gods, the wisest and most powerful of all Gods. Drinking from Mimir's fountain ensured he attained all the knowledge of the universe, but the giant Mimir made him sacrifice an eye first before drinking. First and foremost a war God, Odin lives in and is king of Asgard. As Valfather, he also lives in Valhalla, where the most fearsome warriors go after death in battle. Odin, who often visits Midgard (earth) dressed as an old vagrant, is also a fantastic witch and invented runes, a magically charged set of symbols and the alphabet of the Germanic peoples. He sacrificed himself and hung upside down from the Yggdrasil tree for nine days without food or water, and while there came up with the runes and gave them to the people for spelling and magic. Along with Freya he's considered the greatest practitioner of Shamanism amongst Gods.

Frigg

Frigg is the Goddess of Love, Marriage and Fertility and is Odin's wife, making her a major Goddess of the Aesir. She has sacred knowledge of the destiny of every living being and is said to weave the fate of them all. This is related to the Norse concept of Wyrd, where patterns of the past influence the patterns of the future.

Loki

Loki is the Norse God of Mischief and Strife. He is the half-brother of Odin but is a giant and so a sworn enemy of his half-brother and all the Aesir Gods. Loki started out as a friend to them but often took the giants side in disagreements and so was cast out. Loki can transform into anything and often did to cause distress to the Gods. He once transformed himself into an old hag and tricked Frigg into telling him that the only thing that could kill her son Baldur was mistletoe. He then went to a celebration where Baldur was showing off his strength by allowing people to throw spears at him. Tricking Baldur's blind brother Hod (the God of Dark and Night) he helped guide Hod's spear to Baldur and in doing so used the mistletoe branch to kill him instantly. This, and the murder of Frigg, Odin's wife, meant he and Odin became mortal enemies.

Thor

Thor is the God of Thunder and War and protector of Midgard (earth) and Asgard (heavens). The son of Odin, he is the strongest of the Norse Gods, uses a hammer (moilnir) as his weapon and wears a belt that increases his strength.

Freya

Freya is a Love Goddess of Sex and Promiscuity with a name that translates as Lady. Initially a Goddess of the Vanir, she became an honorary Goddess of the Aesir. Freya is one of the main Goddesses in Wicca as she is also a Goddess of Magic and Divination. She wears a necklace called Brisingamen, forged by dwarves, which makes her irresistible to anyone she wants. Her husband was turned into a horrific sea creature by the Gods and as vengeance she swore to kill all the Norse Gods. After learning magic she set about killing them, but the Gods loved her spirit and made her a Goddess, then gave her husband a place in Valhalla even though he did not die a hero. Freya is called upon for guidance and to help with magic. She is also associated with the faerie realms, and as Goddess is entitled to half the souls that die in battle and go to Valhalla, as she guides them after death.

Hel

Hel, a giantess, is the daughter of Loki and Goddess of the Underworld (Helheim). Half her face is beautiful and half is terribly ugly, whilst the top half of her body is beautiful and the bottom half is dead and rotten. To some this symbolises the light and dark in all of us. But Hel is often a vengeful and hateful Goddess, having been sent by Odin to the underworld for being the ugly daughter of Loki. She is extremely protective of the dead and guards Helheim with great care. Those wishing to receive wisdom or information from the dead, or find loved ones, may find they do not always pass her judgement.

Tyr

Tyr is a War God like Odin and Thor, though he only has one hand as it was bitten off by the wolf Fenrir, son of Loki. When Fenrir was captured he refused to be bound by the Gods unless someone put their hand in his mouth as a symbol of good faith. Tyr was the only God brave enough to do this and his hand was bitten off. He was then renowned by the Gods for his bravery and became a God of Intelligence and Council, as well as Justice and Law.

Baldur

Baldur was the first son of Odin and is God of the Sun and Beauty. Pure, innocent and a great warrior, he was loved by both Gods and man. He had a dream that he was going to be killed and so his mother Frigg insisted everything on earth, sea and sky vow not to hurt him. Everything agreed except mistletoe and when Loki found out about this he tricked Baldur's blind brother Hod into killing him.

In the future, according to Norse legend, there will be a great battle, called Ragnarok, between all the Gods and Goddesses. The nine worlds will be destroyed and the universe devoured. Odin and Loki will fight to the death. Baldur and Hod will then be resurrected and rule the new world in Odin's place.

Celtic Gods and Goddesses

In the beginning there was nothing but the sea, and then a piece of land appeared and when the sea met the land and made froth a white mare was born, made of sea-foam and called Eiocha. On the land a tree grew, born of Eiocha. By eating its berries Eiocha became pregnant and gave birth to the God Cernunnos. While in childbirth Eiocha grabbed at the tree, ripped off some of the bark and threw it into the sea, and this bark turned into the giants of the deep.

Cernunnos watched the giants as they played together, mated and started families. Soon he grew jealous and wanted a family of his own, so he and Eiocha mated and gave birth to the Gods Maponos, Tauranis, and Teutates, as well as the Goddess Epona. After the new Gods had grown Eiocha became disenchanted by the land and wanted to return to the water, so she transformed into Tethra, Goddess of the Sea.

When the Gods of the land became bored, with no subjects to rule over or worship them, they created man from the wood of trees. Cernunnos made wild animals and became their watcher and protector. Teutates created weapons and gave them to man to hunt. Maponos created music and gave man and animals a voice. Tauranis created lightning and thunder and would often throw them to the ground in a thunderous roar so the people and animals would flee in fear.

The giants of the sea saw these Gods being worshipped and loved by their creations and became jealous, so they came together to overthrow the land Gods. Their plan was to flood the land, kill the Gods underwater and take over. Tethra (Eiocha) heard their plans and went onto land to warn her children. And so the Gods were ready for the sea giants when they flooded the lands. They climbed to the top of the oak tree where the water did not reach. Tauranis created lightning like never seen before and aimed them at the sea giants. Maponos sang so loud it broke the sky, which he then hurled at the sea giants causing great asteroids. Teutates took deadly aim with his bow and arrow. This war broke the land into segments. Earth split and the water drained into great seas between the lands. Epona rescued one man, one woman and many animals from the great flood and took them to the safety of Cernunnos Forest, where they mated and created a new race. This new race was the Gods of the Tuatha de Danaan, the first race on earth.

Cernunnos

Cernunnos, also known as Cerne or Herne, is half man, half stag and a consort of the Goddess. God of the Wild Hunt, he rules over all that is wild such as forests, trees, wild animals, flora and fauna. A horned God, he makes love to and marries the Moon Goddess who then gives birth to all things wild in spring and summer. Cernunnos dies and retreats to the underworld and is born again on the winter solstice with the rebirth of the sun.

Angus

Angus is a Scottish God of Love and Beauty. His music is bewitching and draws lovers together, while his kisses are said to turn into singing birds.

Archianrhod

Archianrhod is the Welsh Goddess of the Silver Wheel, a Moon Goddess, the Goddess of Knowledge, Wisdom and Connectedness, especially birth, death and rebirth. She is said to welcome good people to her paradise land of the dead.

Belenos / Bel

Bel is the Celtic Sun God likened to Apollo by the Romans. Shrines for Bel were erected all over England and especially in Cornwall. Bel is the God of Light, Health and Healing, the God who is celebrated on the Sabbat of Beltane, where huge bonfires are made in his honour. The meaning of Beltane roughly translates to 'The fire of the God Bel'.

Lugh

Lugh is a Celtic Sun God, celebrated on the Sabbat of Lughnasadh. He is the Hero God and has been likened to the God Pan.

Beli

Beli is the Sun Goddess. As the female aspect of the sun she mostly represents the healing aspect of the sun's rays and is seen as the more nurturing aspect of the sun.

Brighid

Brighid, also known as Bridie and Brigid, is the Goddess of Poetry, Healing and Crafts. A triple Goddess, she is a crone in autumn and winter, a maiden in spring and a mother in summer. Her breath is said to be the warm air which wakes the flowers in the spring. A fire Goddess usually depicted with flaming red hair, she is celebrated on the Sabbat of Imbolc in February. Worshippers make a four pointed wheel called a Brighid's Cross to honour her.

Ceridwen

Ceridwen is a Goddess of Corn and Grain, a spring Goddess but unlike Brighid a Goddess of late spring. Ceridwen is a great magician and can shape shift. She transformed herself into a hen and by eating a grain of corn gave birth to Taliesen the great poet and bard. Ceridwen is also a mother Goddess and a Goddess of Inspiration and Magic.

Dagda

Dagda is the father God. Ruler of life and death, he carries a magic club that with one strike can kill nine men, but with a handle that can bring anyone back to life. Also known as 'The Dagda' he keeps the seasons in order by playing a magic harp. Father of Brighid and a high king of the Tuatha de Danaan, he is said to mate with Goddess Morrigan on the sabbat Samhain.

Danu

Also known as Ani and Aine, Danu is the mother Goddess of the Tuatha de Danaan, which literally translates to 'Children of Danu.' She was said to have birthed all things into being, including the universe and all the Gods, and is believed to be everywhere in every living organism. She is also seen as an Earth Goddess who inspires and loves music and creativity.

Morrigan

Morrigan is the Goddess of Death, War, Fate and Fertility. She was a high Goddess to the Tuatha de Danaan, was consort to The Dagda and weaves fate, much like Frigg the Norse Goddess. She is associated with death and can give warriors super strength in battle and, appearing as a raven or crow with a cloak of black wings, she announces the death of fallen warriors. She was said to have been seen by a lake or river as a beautiful woman washing the bloodied clothes of the soldiers who would die in battle. Morrigan is a symbol of female empowerment, with the fate of every person in her hands.

A Reference Guide to Gods and Goddesses

Roman Gods and Goddesses

Apollo - God of the Sun

Bacchus - God of Wine

Ceres - The Earth Goddess

Cupid - God of Love

Diana - Goddess of the Moon and Hunting

Flora - Goddess of Flowers

Janus - God of Doors

Juno - Queen of the Gods

Jupiter - King of the Gods

Maia - Goddess of Growth

Mars - God of War

Mercury - Messenger of the Gods

Minerva - Goddess of Wisdom

Neptune - God of the Sea

Pluto - God of Death

Plutus - God of Wealth

Proserpine - Goddess of the Underworld and Spring

Saturn - God of Time

Uranus and Gaia - Parents of Saturn

Venus - Goddess of Love

Vesta - Goddess of the Home

Vulcan - The Smith God

Greek Gods and Goddesses

Aphrodite - Goddess of Love

Apollo - God of Music and Medicine

Ares - God of War

Artemis - Goddess of the Hunt

Athena - Goddess of Wisdom

Demeter - Goddess of the Harvest

Dionysus - God of Wine

Eros - God of Love

Gaia - Goddess of Earth

Hades - God of the Underworld

Hephaistos - God of Smithing

Hera - Goddess of Marriage

Hermes - Messenger of the Gods

Persephone - Goddess of Underworld and of Spring

Poseidon - God of the Sea

Zeus - King of Gods

Egyptian Gods and Goddesses

Ammu - Devoured those souls judged unworthy of the Afterlife

Amun - Creator God, later coupled with Ra to make the God Amun Ra

Anqet - Goddess of Water and Lust

Anubis   - God of the Dead and Embalming

Atum - Creator God later became Ra-Atum, he represented the evening Sun

Bast - Goddess of the Home, Protection and Children. Cat Goddess

Bes - God of Music, Dance, War and Slaughter

Duamutef - God of Disease

Geb - God of the Earth and guide to heaven

Hapi - Nile God

Hathor - Goddess of Love, Happiness, Dance and Music; Protector of Women

Horus - God of the Sun and Magic

Isis - Goddess of the Moon, Love, Fertility and Magic

Khensu - God of the Moon

Ma'at - Goddess of Knowledge, Law, Order and Truth

Min - God of Fertility in Men

Mut - Goddess of the Earth

Neith - Goddess of War

Nut - Goddess of the Skies

Osiris - God of Earth and Vegetation

Ptah - God of Crafts

Ra - God of the Sun and Sky

Satet - Goddess of the Nile

Sekhmet - Goddess of War and Destruction

Selket - Goddess of Scorpions and Magic

Seshat - Goddess of Writing and Measurement

Set - God of the Night Sky

Shu - God of Space and the Universe

Tawaret - Goddess of Pregnancy and Childbirth

Tefnut - Goddess of Rain, Water and Sky

Thoth   - God of Wisdom and Learning

Norse Gods and Goddesses

Aegir - God of the Sea

Alaisiagae - Goddess of War

Balder - God of Light, Strength and Beauty

Eir - Goddess of Healing with Herbs

Elli - Crone Goddess of Old Age

Forseti - God of Justice

Freya - Goddess of Fertility, Sex and the Moon

Frey - God of Sun and Rain, Peace and War, and the Harvest

Frigg - Goddess of Love, Fertility, Marriage and Motherhood

Gefion - Goddess of Vegetation and Fertility

Gerd - Goddess of the Earth

Gullveig - Goddess of Sorcery, Prophecy and Healing

Heimdall - God of Light and Guardian of the Rainbow Bridge

Hel - Goddess of Death and the Underworld

Hermod - Messenger God

Hodr - God of Winter and Darkness

Hoenu - God of Silence

Iduna - Goddess of Eternal Youth

Jord - Goddess of the Earth

Loki - Norse trickster God

Nanna - Goddess of the New Moon and Fertility

Nerthus - Goddess of Witchcraft, Magic and Spells

Njord - God of the Winds, Sea, Fire, and Wealth

Odin - King of the Norse Gods

Ran - Goddess of Storms and Water

Saga - Goddess of Memory

Sif - Goddess of Corn

Sjofna - Goddess of Love

Skadi - Goddess of Winter and Hunting

Thor - God of Thunder and War

Uller - God of Hunting and Glory also a God of Winter

Var - Goddess of Agreements

Vidar - God of Vengeance

Weland - God of Smiths and Metalworkers

Celtic Gods and Goddesses

Aine - Goddess associated with the Summer Solstice, Goddess of Crops and Cattle

Aerten - Goddess of Fate, presided over the outcome of war between several Celtic clans

Aife - Goddess of Protection and Teaching

Airmid - Goddess of Medicine

Angus - God of Beauty and Love

Anu - Goddess of Fertility, Love and Protection

Arawn - God of the Underworld, Vengeance and Reincarnation

Arianrhod - Goddess of the Silver wheel, Fortune Telling and Fate

Baile - God of Speech, Intelligence and Mental Activity

Ban - Goddess of Childbirth

Bel – God of Fire, the Sun and Success

Belisama - Goddess of Light and Fire, the Sun and Crafting

Blodeuwedd - Goddess of Flowers

Breasal - God of Protection, especially for those travelling

Bran - God of Prophecies

Brid - Goddess of Fire, Imagination and Crafting

Caer Ibormeith - Goddess of Sleep and Dreams

Caillech - Goddess of Curses, Disease and Plague

Cebhfhionn – Goddess of Knowledge.

Cernunnos - God of Animals, everything Wild and Woodlands

Cerridwen - Goddess of death and Regeneration

Creiddylad - Goddess of Strength of Will

Coventina - Goddess of Divination

Cred - Faery Queen Goddess

Cromm Cruaich - God of Death and contacting the dead

The Dagda - God of Death and Rebirth

Diancecht - God of Healing

Damara - Goddess of Fertility.

Danu (also Dana) - Goddess of Magic

Eadon - Goddess of Poetry and Creativity

Queen of Elphame - Goddess of Death

Epona - Goddess of Horses

Eri of the Golden Hair - Goddess of the Moon

Flidais - Goddess of Forests and Wild Creatures

Goibniu - God of Smithing

Grainne - Goddess of Herbs

Gwydion - God of Enchantment and Magic

Lassair - Goddess of Midsummer

Latis - Goddess of Water and Beer

LeFay - Goddess of the Sea and Healing

Llyr - God of the Sea and Water

Macha - Goddess of Female Power

Manannan - God of the Seas, of Storms and Weather at Sea

Morrigan - shapeshifting Goddess of War, Magic and Death

Rosmerta - Goddess of Healing

Scathach - Goddess of Prophecy, Protection, and Teaching

Somhlth - God of Men and Male Prowess

Taliesin - God of Magic and Knowledge

White Lady - Goddess of Death, Destruction and Annihilation

"To see the world in a grain of sand,
and to see heaven in a wild flower,
hold infinity in the palm of your hands,
and eternity in an hour"
William Blake

Nature

Nature is all important. But nature is not simply plants and trees, it is everything; the ocean, the sky, the stars, the sun and moon. We are nature and everything is natural, for we would not exist if it were not for nature. It is the air we breathe, the ground we walk upon, the food we eat, the stars at night. Wicca is a nature based religion and so we live our lives in accordance with nature. Our holidays fall on the seasons, the solstices and the equinox. To be Wiccan is to love nature, and as balance is crucial to nature, so it is to Wicca. We strive to find a balance in our lives. We embrace our dark side as well as our light, for it is just as much a part of us as light is, and to not do this would be dangerous, as it would isolate our darkness. But of course, we do not give darkness precedence, for this is dangerous to. Instead, we hold both together, balanced. We embrace our own femininity and masculinity, whatever our gender. We have a God and a Goddess and we strive to live our lives in harmony with nature.

Wiccans have four seasonal holidays:

Samhain - Winter

Imbolc - Spring

Beltane - Summer

Lammas - Autumn

We also have four major holidays celebrated on the Spring and Autumn Equinox and on the Summer and Winter Solstice:

Yule - Winter Solstice

Ostara - Spring Equinox

Litha - Summer Solstice

Mabon - Autumn Equinox

All together these are called the eight Sabbats. To find out more about these please refer to the chapter on the Sabbats. Wiccans also follow moon phases throughout the year and practice our rituals and magic using the power of the moon. There is more on this in the chapter on Esbats.

To get in touch with nature, go for long walks in the countryside, in woodland or on the beach. Pay attention to your surroundings; look at the trees and how they transform at the changing of the seasons, look at the different plants, their smells, their colours, their beauty. Feel and smell the earth and the grass. Bury your feet in the sand at the beach. Walk along river banks and notice the shrubs. See if you can identify them, look at them close up, *really* look at them. Attention to detail is not just being particular; it's something great poets and artists do, and yet it's inherent in all of us – it's natural, like the creativity and love within us all. Look up to the stars. Be amazed that we are all made from the same matter, whether we be animal, plant or mineral.

Learn about the different rocks and crystals, trees, plants and herbs, the different animals and their role and habits within this great cycle of life. Listen to nature, listen to the wind and the trees, listen to the birds singing and other animals chatting and calling out their warnings and mating calls. Listen to the rain. Smell the grass and mud after a good rainfall. Close your eyes and tune into the sound of the earth. Listen to a flowing river or the waves at the beach. How does all this make you feel? Breathe it in and smile. We were born with five senses; some might even say six. And yet modern society can take us away from all that is natural, both within us and without. Help yourself and you help us all appreciate and reclaim what is natural, because we are all connected.

Nature harnesses so much power. Inside every one of us is an enormous amount of power; we can mix ingredients together to make a bomb that can devastate a whole city, the whole world itself. We can build crafts that can fly. We can cure disease, build cities and erect monuments. As humans we have untold power within each one of us, using the tools and ingredients nature has provided for us. Let's use it for the right purposes, to celebrate our being part of nature, not our dominance over it.

In science, within the last hundred years or so, they have discovered infra-red, ultra-violet, x-ray, radio waves, electricity and so much more. Just because these things can be explained, does it make them any less magic? These are things that were once hidden from the naked eye. What is science going to discover next? Some people say witchcraft is just magic that science hasn't discovered yet.

We have created telephones that allow us to speak to people at the other end of the world, and now we have the internet and smartphones with their incredible fast-moving technology. It's amazing, isn't it, when you stop and think about it? But remember, these things are accomplished by using the power of the earth, using metals, generated electricity and other natural earth resources. We are just beginning to understand solar power and other natural energy resources. We understand so little about our own minds. There really is so much more out there.

Medicine is just another name for potions, a mixture of ingredients used for effect, whether that is to heal, give energy, induce coma, anesthetise, hallucinate, make you tell the truth or help you feel euphoric. They are all potions, and 'witches' were the first to put these ingredients together, to understand all this. It is where medicine was born. We were the first to use natural power for cause and effect. Shamans, witches and witch doctors were the first medical people and scientist. The vast majority of medicine that the Western world 'discovers' has been used by indigenous tribes for thousands of years. Wicca means wise or wise one. We never stop learning and discovering more about nature and its incredible power.

*"Love is the affinity which links and draws together
the elements of the world... Love, in fact, is the
agent of universal synthesis."*

Pierre Teilhard de Chardin

The Elements

Wiccans work with the five elements; Earth, Air, Fire, Water and Spirit. Without any one of these elements, the building blocks of life, we would not exist. Wiccans use these elements on altars when we call on them to combine and give power to our spells. We honour them for giving us life and for giving us nature.

Each of these elements has its own attributes and magical properties:

Earth is stability, strength and healing. It is connected to practicality and finance, but also to beauty and nature. Earth element is feminine. To use magic with this element, use herbs for healing, or flowers and trees. Bury objects, notes and symbols within the earth itself.

Air is intelligence and creativity, independence and thought. The Air element represents deep consciousness and psychic power, inspiration and imagination. You cannot see Air but it is always there. To do magic using Air, a masculine element, use incense or aromatherapy oils. Write a message on paper and give it to the wind. Magic representing Air is about travelling, freedom, knowledge and finding things that were once lost.

Fire is ambition, passion and forward moving. It represents energy and getting things done and is the element that brings love and heat. Fire represents change or transformation and is the element of magic. When using this masculine element in magic, light candles, burn objects in fires and use cookery.

Water is spiritual and ever changing, connected to our emotions and subconscious. Strong when moving, but calm and still when dormant, it is a purifier and gives us wisdom of the soul. To do magic with this feminine element brew teas using herbs, relax in herbal baths, submerge objects and symbols under water, use water to purify, add sea salt to water or use seawater as a holy water to purify a space or object.

Spirit is the prime element that is present in everything. It provides the space and balance for all the other elements to exist. It is the universe, gravity, and what all things are made of. It is our being and our soul. To do magic using the spirit element you should combine all the other elements in your magical working. This would usually be done when you are trying to see the future, communicate with the spirit world or for deep meditation.

We give thanks to these elements at our altars and use their power in our spell work and rituals. In Wicca remember, we work with balance. It's been written in this book a number of times already but it is always worth repeating. This balance is everywhere, or should be, and includes elemental balance. When writing this book I am working with the Air element. Someone wanting to work with their aggression, frustration or passion should work with the Fire element. But people often use one element more than the others and can become over dependent on one element or have trouble relating to others. We must find a balance and use each element equally to stay focused and balanced within ourselves.

The elements also connect to other parts of our life and surroundings and these are important when conducting our rituals and spell work.

Earth is North, Air is East, Fire is South and Water is West.

We can use various things to represent an element for our altars. Below are some suggestions. For further information on how to set up your altar, please see the chapter on Altars on page 74.

To represent Earth In the north quarter of our altar we would use salt, rocks, crystals, stones, acorns, tree branches, flowers, herbs, and a green or brown candle.

To represent Air in the east quarter of our altars we would use burning incense, feathers or a yellow candle.

To represent Fire in the south quarter of our altars we would use a burning candle, or a red or orange candle.

To represent Water in the west quarter of our altars we would use a glass or goblet of water, sea shells, sea weed, river water or a blue candle.

To represent Spirit in the centre of our altars we would use a pentagram which brings all the elements together, or we can also use a white candle.

Additionally, each of the twelve signs of the Zodiac correspond to the four main elements:

Earth signs are Taurus, Capricorn and Virgo.

Air signs are Aquarius, Libra and Gemini.

Fire signs are Leo, Aries and Sagittarius.

Water signs are Cancer, Scorpio and Pisces.

For further information on Astrology please see the chapter on Sun Sign Astrology on page 183.

Finally, the four suits of the tarot cards symbolise the four elements in the following way:

Pentacles represent career and money and symbolise Earth

Swords represent thought and intelligence and symbolise Air

Wands represent dreams and ambition and symbolise Fire.

Cups represent relationships and emotions and symbolise Water.

"There is nothing so wise as a circle"
Rainer Maria Rilke

The Great Wheel

Almost everything in the universe is a circle and a cycle. Nothing ever stays the same and yet nothing ever *really* changes either. Of course there is change, there is constant change, but when we look at the bigger picture we can see these changes are actually repetitions, part of the natural cycle of life. And so everything turns in a cycle; the seasons, the moon, the earth around the sun, the cycle of life and death, the cycle of plant life.

Our pagan ancestors knew the significance of the circle and created many of their worshipping monuments as wooden or stone circles. There are many of these pagan monuments still standing, especially in Britain and Europe, with the most famous being Stonehenge. Others however, are just as impressive and important and don't have flocks of tourists around them. How could anyone not be amazed by a visit to Castlerigg Stone Circle in Cumbria, with its 360 degree view of the surrounding fells and mountains? Find out if there are any stone circles near you and spend some time there. Feel the energy that emanates from those stones, heaved into place thousands of years ago but created by mother earth herself millions of years before.

The circle in Wicca can be cut into four to represent the four seasons or the four elements (the centre being spirit). It can be cut into eight pieces to represent the eight Sabbats, and it can be cut into twelve pieces to represent the twelve signs of the zodiac or the twelve full moons of the year (sometimes thirteen if there are two full moons within the same month). All together these make The Great Wheel.

The Great Wheel is the circle of time, the circle of the year, the circle of life, death and rebirth. And as the Great Wheel turns, another cycle or phase has also turned, until it comes full circle and starts once more.

The Sabbats are called the Wheel of the Year. In Wicca time is seen more as a never ending circle than a straight timeline that moves towards a final end. When we are born our journey on the great wheel begins. There is a saying in Wicca: "What has been will be again."

51

Sabbats

The Sabbats are eight sun-related festivals that fall on the four seasons of the year; the winter and summer solstice and the spring and autumn equinox. Each year the sun waxes and wanes. On the winter solstice the sun starts waxing, the days become longer and colder and the earth turns and finally starts to warm again. Plants grow, animals mate, fruits starts ripening and the earth is full of nature's bounty, until it reaches its climax on the summer solstice. Then the sun starts waning and eventually plants start to die, trees lose their leaves, nights get longer and the coldness sets in. In Celtic belief, which most of the Sabbats are named after, the story of the great battle between the Holly King and the Oak King ensues every year. The Oak King represents the light and is sometimes known as the God of Light. The Holly King represents the dark. Both are as important as each other as one could not exist without the other. The Triple Goddess meanwhile, goes through three stages throughout the year; the maiden, the mother and the crone. This represents not only the three stages of a woman's life, all of which should be embraced and appreciated, but also a balancing counterpart to the Horned God and a reflection on nature itself.

These Sabbats help us tune into and celebrate nature. They are a time to thank the Gods and Goddesses for what we have. The Sabbats were celebrated by the Celts in ancient times but have since been adopted by Pagans and Wiccans worldwide. Northern and southern hemispheres have the Sabbats at different times of course, because the seasons are different on each hemisphere.

There are four fire festivals known as Major Sabbats:

Samhain (Winter)
Northern Hemisphere, October 31st and Southern Hemisphere May 1st

Imbolc (Spring)
Northern Hemisphere, February 1st and Southern Hemisphere, August 1st

Beltane (Summer)
Northern Hemisphere, April 30th to May 1st and Southern Hemisphere, October 31st

Lughnasadh/Lammas (Autumn)
Northern Hemisphere, August 1st and Southern Hemisphere, February 2nd

These were called fire festivals because in ancient times the festivals would be celebrated by burning a huge bonfire in the centre of a town or village and all the townsfolk would gather to drink and be merry with a big feast prepared to honour the Sun Gods. The word 'bonfire' comes from the Celts. After a great feast any leftover bones would be sacrificially thrown into the fire to make a bone fire. All the villagers then lit a torch from the bone fire and took it home to light their fireplaces as this would expel any negativity from their homes.

The four lesser Sabbats are celebrated on the solstice and equinox. Summer solstice is the longest day of the year, while winter solstice is the longest night. The two equinoxes occur when night and day are both of equal lengths.

The lesser Sabbats are:

Yule (Winter Solstice)
Northern Hemisphere, December 19th to 22nd and Southern Hemisphere, June 20th to 23rd

Ostara (Spring Equinox)
Northern Hemisphere, March 19th to 22nd and Southern Hemisphere, September 20th to 23rd

Litha (Summer Solstice)
Northern Hemisphere, June 19th to 22nd and Southern Hemisphere, December 20th to 23rd

Mabon (Autumn Equinox)
Northern Hemisphere, September 19th to 22nd and Southern Hemisphere, March 20th to 23rd

Below is a list of each Sabbat and its meaning. Every Sabbat is a time to celebrate nature, to have family and friends around for feasts, and to light fires in honour of the Sun Gods and Goddesses.

Samhain (pronounced Sow-en) - October 31st

The word Samhain means 'summer's end'. Primarily a Celtic festival, Samhain is the Wiccan New Year as the wheel of the year has turned full circle. It is a festival of the dead, a time when the veil between the world of spirits and the human world is at its thinnest. Samhain is a marking of the onset of winter, when leaves are falling from the trees in great droves and plant life is starting to descend deep into the earth making it seem bare and barren. This is a time when the Sun God, or the Horned God who is keeper of the forest and wild animals, also descends to the underworld to sleep. As he descends, the veil between the two worlds is thinned and we can commune with lost loved ones.

Earth starts to draw energy inwards instead of outwards. Appropriately, this is a time for us to draw our energies inwards too, a time of contemplation to think about the year that we have just had, to draw on any successes or mistakes and learn from them ready for the coming new year. At Samhain we remember our ancestors and loved ones who've passed away. We should adorn our altars with pictures of people or pets we would like to remember and give thanks for having them in our lives. We also put seasonal fruit and vegetables, such as apples, pumpkins and fallen leaves, on our altars to honour the season. It is a time of endings but is also a time of new beginnings; as the wheel has turned we say goodbye to things past and prepare for things anew.

Samhain is the third harvest festival; Lughnasadh being the first and Mabon the second. While the other two are festivals of crop harvests and fruits Samhain is a harvest of flesh. In ancient times it would have been a time when cattle were slaughtered and stored for the long winter months ahead.

The triple Goddess is in her crone phase. She is the wise one, or the dark mother who swallows up the Oak King (Horned God) in her womb (the underworld) but will give birth to him again at Yule. No flowers will bloom but the earth is filled with warm soothing colours such as blacks, browns and oranges, the colours of this Sabbat.

Yule

Yule is the winter solstice, when we celebrate the rebirth of the Sun, or the various other names he's known by: the Horned God, The Green Man, The Oak King and the God of Light. It is the longest night of the year, but the nights after winter solstice will start to lessen and days will become longer as the sun grows in strength.

There is a battle between light and dark on this day and light will prevail as the Holly King (the dark God of the waning sun) is defeated by the Oak King (The Horned God, God of the waxing sun) The Goddess has given birth to the Oak King, who's light is so strong it defeats the Holly King and sends him down to the underworld where he will nurse his wounds and rest until they do battle again on Litha (summer solstice). By giving birth to the Oak King, the Goddess, who is in her crone phase and very weak after a long year, will die, but she will be reborn again as a young maiden at Imbolc.

On Yule we give thanks to the Goddess for her sacrifice and for bringing back the waxing sun who will bestow many gifts upon the earth in the months to come. We celebrate by encouraging the sun to rise and grow in power and we do this by remembering times when we had plenty. We enjoy rich foods, drink and enjoy a big feast and light fires. We give gifts to each other to show our appreciation and celebrate having loved ones in our lives.

At Yule we adorn our homes and altars with evergreens to show that amidst death and infertility the earth is still alive and growing. It is customary to place an evergreen tree in the home and decorate it with offerings, particularly those that are shiny and represent the sun. We also decorate with nuts, pine cones, dried fruit and ornaments of seasonal animals such as Robins. Because holly and mistletoe bare berries at this time of year we decorate our homes with them. The white seeds of the mistletoe represent semen of the Gods and the red berries of the holly represent the blood of the Goddesses, symbolising the re-joining of male and female. Sprigs from holly trees were worn in the hair during rituals performed by the priests of the Celts, the Druids, at summer and winter solstice, as the sharp leaves protect the wearer against evil spirits.

Imbolc (pronounced Imolk)

The word Imbolc means 'in the belly.' We see the first sign that spring has arrived; seeds and shrubs begin to appear; animals come out from hibernation. This is a time to celebrate the waxing sun, its longer days and the promise of what is still to come. We make a fire in honour of the Sun God and burn any wood or trees that are left over from Yule, then bury the ashes.

In Celtic times the day was Bride's Day or Brigid's Day, which refers to the Celtic Triple Goddess. People would decorate their homes with a Brigid's cross, often made from straw and sometimes called a sun wheel or wheel of fire. They were said to bring good luck for the spring harvest and to homes that exhibited them. It is also traditional to make corn dollies at this time, to welcome the Goddess back into your home and bless it. Some also make a Brigid's Bed from a small wooden basket or cardboard box, put the corn dolly in the bed and then lay it at their fireplace to encourage Goddess Brigid to spend the night and bless their home.

At Imbolc we should start to make plans for the year ahead, asking ourselves what we want to achieve and how we are going to achieve it. Plant the seeds of any future plans at this time and watch them grow over the coming months. Figure out what you need to be happy and take the first steps to achieving this, whether this is a new job, new house, new love, losing weight or giving up an addiction. Put this into action at Imbolc.

At Imbolc the Triple Goddess is reborn as the maiden, the young fertile earth. We adorn our altars with bright colours such as yellows and whites, alongside a Brigid's Cross. This is an excellent time for doing meditation at your altar and contemplating the year ahead. It is also an excellent time for tarot reading or any kind of divination workings, to see what the future has in store.

Ostara / Eostre

Ostara is the spring equinox, a time when night and day are at equal lengths. It is named after the Anglo Saxon Goddess of Eostre, also known as Ostara. The Anglo Saxon month which became April was called Eastermonath. The Goddess Eostre is a fertility Goddess and her symbols are the egg and rabbit, representing new life, fertility and mating.

The days grow lighter and warmer and the young Horned God and Goddess flirt with each other. This is a time when the earth is full of fertility; new flowers and crops are shooting up everywhere, rising from their winter months in the underworld. Energies are pushed outward onto the earth again. Equilibrium and harmony are what we seek, as the equinox is a time to find balance between our light and dark sides, to go deep within ourselves and learn to love our imperfections as well as our strengths. Look at your inner masculine and feminine qualities. If you find that you are out of balance, your dark side is stronger than your light. If your negativity is overtaking your positivity then try to realign the balance through meditation. Ask yourself why they are out of balance and try to put right what you feel is wrong.

This is a time to honour the Goddesses Ishtar and Persephone, risen once more from the underworld so that the earth can recover from its barren spell. Trees become greener. Daffodils and daisies flourish. Birds sing joyfully in the trees while bees and wasps come back. We adorn our altars with springtime flowers, with painted eggs and bunnies to give thanks for the spring and the wakening earth.

Beltane

Beltane, the beginning of summer, is a Celtic fire festival. In Irish Gaelic Beltane means May but it is also associated with the Celtic god Bel, a God of light and fire, the Greek god Apollo, the Roman God Sol Invictus, the Norse God Sol and the Egyptian God Horus.

This is a time of fertility, when the Triple Goddess in her maiden form will marry and mate with the Horned God or the Green Man as he is often called. It is a magical union that ensures the fertility of the earth. Beltane is also a time of Handfasting (Pagan Marriage). The Maypole is a tradition on May 1st. The pole, decorated with plants and flowers, represents the male penis while the strings or streams around the top represent the Goddess. Young maidens take a stream and dance around the maypole, wrapping the streams around the pole.

Communities came together after a long cold winter. Fires were built to honour the sun and people jumped over them; young unmarried people for a wish of marriage; young wives to ensure fertility and couples to strengthen a bond. It is customary to make flower garlands to wear on your head and daisy chains to wear as a necklace. This will honour the Faerie folk as this is their day of celebration too.

Beltane is a celebration of the union between God and Goddess, when the sun is strong and the earth is bearing gifts. It is a time of wine and merriment. On our altars we put branches of the hawthorn tree to honour the Goddess. Add flowers and wine as offerings. Make a feast and invite family and friends to join in the celebrations, hold parties, dance and enjoy the day.

Litha

Litha is the summer solstice, the longest day of the year, when the sun is at its brightest and strongest. The God has risen and fought off darkness to ensure the fertility of the land, but by doing this he has also brought about his own demise. He does this for the love of the Goddess, and to keep her earth fertile he has sown his seeds and made the earth rich.

The dark lord, the Holly King, is the God of the waning sun. Some say he is the dark aspect of the Horned God, the Oak King. Others say he is the twin of the Horned God. One was born of dark and the other of lightness. Each year they battle for supremacy of the skies. On Litha the dark lord Holly King will win the battle and the God of Light the Oak King will descend into the underworld. The Holly King will rule the skies until Yule when the Oak King is reborn with light so strong it banishes the dark lord Holly King back into the underworld.

On this day though, the Oak King is weak because he has shone so brightly for so long. He is defeated by the Holly King and starts his descent into the underworld. This is still a joyous time though, for The Oak King has fertilised the earth and the Goddess is heavily pregnant with the harvest to come. Flowers are everywhere, mature and ready for pollination, but once they have had their pollination they will begin to die so that their seeds and fruits can develop in the following year. Summer fruits will be abundant at this time but only for a short period.

This is a time when we are carefree and can relax and enjoy the love and fruits of the earth, but we also take into account the death of the Horned God the Oak King and say hello to the Holly King, the dark lord rising. Fires lit on Litha are said to possess magical powers; you can make wishes into the flames or write your hopes on paper and toss them into the fire in the hope they will come to fruition. Use bright solar colours such as orange, red and gold. Circles, discs and Brigid's Crosses as well as fruits, vegetables and flowers can go on your altar.

Try and find a spot where the sunlight floods into your home. Ask the Holly King to give us a good winter.

Lughnasadh (pronounced loo-nas-saa)

Lughnasadh, or Lammas as it is also known, is a fire festival, one of three harvest festivals, and is celebrated on the first day of autumn. The Anglo Saxon name Lammas means 'Loaf Mass' as it was a time for making bread on the wheat harvest. Lughnasadh is the name given to this festival in honour of the Celtic Sun God Lugh, a fire God of crafts and skills who presides over the harvest. Lammas is a time to celebrate the earth and its bounty during the harvest. It is also a time to celebrate the fullness of life. We thank the Goddess for the harvest she has bestowed upon us and the sacrifice of the Horned God (The Oak king).

This is a time when the sun is still hot and we can enjoy its energy and light. It is a time of celebration to be happy for our blessings. Stay away from negative thoughts on this day and instead give thanks for what we have, no matter how small. Show gratitude for friends, family, your home and our earth, in fact anything good in your life. Adorn your altar with harvest plants, and with bread and wine to offer to the Goddess. This is a time to make corn dollies and other crafts using wheat and corn. It is a time to start reaping what we have sown, putting into motion what we started at the beginning of the year.

Mabon

Mabon, named after the Welsh God Mabon, is the autumn equinox, a time of balance when both day and night are of the same length. The opposite of spring equinox Ostara, this time we say goodbye to the sun and get ready for cold long nights. This is the last day The Horned God (The Oak King) will spend upon earth before descending into the underworld. The dark Lord of the waning sun (The Holly King) is about to take over.

Modron, meaning 'divine mother', is the Triple Goddess, maiden, mother and crone, usually depicted as all three sitting upon a throne, who gave birth to the God Mabon. Mabon, which means son of the mother, is the healer, God of the underworld and protector of earth, also depicted as the Green Man. The Triple Goddess, Mother of the Harvest, The Goddess still in her mother phase, is still giving birth to earthly fruits.

Mabon, the second of the harvest festivals, is the time to celebrate the benefits of the summer just gone and congratulate ourselves for the work put in during the year. We should look into ourselves and our own balance, realign ourselves. Look at your life, see what is missing or needed, consider how to achieve this change and take the first positive steps. Meditate at your altar on questions you may have. This is the month of the vine, when fruits are ripe and ready to be picked. Give thanks for the bountiful spring and summer but be aware the earth is becoming barren and the cold is coming. Gather fruit and nuts, the Goddesses children. Adorn your altar with them to give thanks to the Gods and Goddess for their gifts. We also ask the Holly King to be kind and gentle with us through the long cold winter months.

Esbats

The word Esbat comes from the Old French word s'esbattre, which means 'to joyfully celebrate.' While Sabbats commemorate the male deity of the sun, Esbats celebrate the female deity of the moon. These are times to do magical workings because the moon is at full power. Leave your magical tools, crystals and jewellery out in the moonlight to cleanse and charge them with psychic energy.

The moon is seen as the ultimate feminine, the Goddess, because its cycles correspond with menstrual cycles. It controls our sea and ocean tides, the blood of the earth, and goes through a waxing and a waning period in every cycle. On the waxing phase we ask for good and positive to come into our lives and when the moon is waning we expel negatives. We give thanks to the great Goddess of the Moon on these nights, and charge our psychic powers by her moonlight. Covens meet on Esbats to perform rituals depending on which branch of Wicca the coven represents. This usually consists of the coven's High Priestess taking the Goddess into her and rituals being performed around this.

A new moon, in darkness and not observable from earth, is the best time to start new projects and put plans into action. Try to accomplish these tasks by the coming full moon and then give thanks to the God and Goddess on this Esbat. There are usually twelve Esbats throughout the year but sometimes there are thirteen if a full moon occurs twice in one month. If this happens we call the second full moon of the month a blue moon. Below is a list and brief description of the Esbats.

January - Wolf Moon Ψ Old Moon Ψ After-Yule Moon

January's full moon is a time of contemplation. The Triple Goddess is in her crone phase. It is still very cold and deep in winter, but the days are starting to become ever so slightly longer. Contemplate your goals and the year ahead, meditate at your altar and ask the Goddess to help you in any new ventures or goals you have set yourself. Use this full moon to charge yourself with energy and strength for the coming year. Perform spell work for protection, luck, happiness and prosperity. Look deep within yourself and ask what you really want from your life and how you can achieve it. The colours associated with this full moon are blacks, whites and silvers. Adorn your altar with nuts, seeds, basil, thyme and marjoram as offerings to ensure a good month ahead. Use crystals hematite, snow obsidian and quartz for healing.

February - Storm Moon Ψ Hunger Moon Ψ Snow Moon Ψ Quickening Moon

February is a time to sow the seeds of any new plans you have for the coming year. Write them down, put them on your altar and ask the Goddess to help you achieve them. This is the time to do magic for strength, fertility and ambition. It is a perfect time to start or try something new. In February we should be thinking in terms of our energy. Are we happy? And if not, then why is this? It is important to feel good in your own skin; if you are not happy then the people around you will not be happy and this brings a circle of negativity into your life. But when you are happy and confident others around you will feel happy and more comfortable in your company. You must put yourself first, so you can keep yourself healthy and happy. This enables you to help and be there for your family and loved ones. Do spell work on this night that helps your health and erases any negativity with the coming waning moon. Colours of this moon are purple and blue, and you should adorn your altar with hyssop, sage and myrrh. Use crystals rose quartz, amethyst and jasper for healing.

March - Chaste Moon Ψ Worm Moon Ψ Crow Moon Ψ Crust Moon Ψ Sugar Moon Ψ Sap Moon

March is the time we welcome spring, a time of cleaning and cleansing, hence the term 'spring clean.' But it's a time to clean ourselves spiritually as well as our homes. After giving your home a good clear out, get a smudge stick (see rituals chapter) and cleanse your home of all negative energy. Put sage, lemongrass or rosemary on your altar as an offering to the Goddess and ask her for blessings over your home and family. March's full moon is a time of high emotions and changes; don't fight them, let them come, but steer the changes in the direction you wish them to go. Look at your finances this month and try to achieve any related goals. Colours of this full moon are greens, yellows and lavenders. Adorn your altar with herbs, high john, betony and basil. Use bloodstone and aquamarine for healing.

April - Seed Moon Ψ Pink Moon Ψ Spring Moon Ψ Egg Moon Ψ Grass Moon Ψ Fish Moon

April is a time of wind and rain. On this Esbat it's a good time to 'draw down the moon' (see rituals chapter) and take the energy of the moon into yourself. Meditate at your altar and thank the Goddess for the gifts that have been bestowed upon you. April is a time to look at your career and work. Ask yourself if you are happy at work and if not, what can you do to improve the situation? Ask the Goddess to help you in seeking your ambitions. This full moon you will be charged with the growing energy of nature and this can hit you in two ways; you will either get very emotional and feel all over the place, in which case you should realign your emotions by meditating and looking at your positives; or you will feel very powered and full of ambition, in which case this is a gift, don't waste it, use the energy to get what you need, be it a job, promotion, starting a business or a new love life. Use candle magic tonight. Colours of this full moon are reds, yellows and blues. Adorn your altar with dandelions, daisies and buttercups. Use crystals quartz, selenite and agate for healing.

May - Hare Moon Ψ Flower Moon Ψ Milk Moon Ψ Corn Planting Moon

May heralds the official start of summer. Adorn your altar with flowers and scents, call on the elements and thank them for their life giving properties. This is a brilliant time for doing magic for improving finances or finding new love, and if you already have a lover then do magic on strengthening the bond. Look at your relationships with family and friends and ask is there anything that can be done to improve these relationships. Ask the Goddess for help and guidance in achieving this. The May full moon asks us to look at the beauty that is around us, the growing and blooming earth. The colours of this full moon are reds, oranges and yellows. Adorn your altar with flowers, and with cinnamon and mint as offerings. Use stones amber and garnet for healing.

June - Strawberry Moon Ψ Dyad Moon Ψ Rose Moon Ψ Hot Moon

The days are hot and long with a scattering of showers, the scent of flowers is in the air and the fields are lush and green. The Goddess is in her mother phase and tending the earth. This is the perfect time to relax and be grateful to the God and Goddess for their work in fertilizing and sustaining the land. It would be a good time to do an outside Esbat, gazing up at the stars, or to do a 'drawing down of the moon' ritual to energize your psychic powers. June is a time of loving yourself; if there is something you don't like about yourself, ask what you can do to change this. Appeal to the Goddess for guidance in helping you improve and feel more confident. Colours of this full moon are golds, yellows and oranges. Adorn your altar with parsley, mugwort and moss. Use Topaz and lapis lazuli for healing.

July - Mead Moon Ψ Buck Moon Ψ Hay Moon Ψ Thunder Moon

The July full moon is a great time to do spell work regarding career, stamina, love and beauty. At this time of year the earth is abundant with herbs, flowers and scents, so incorporate this on your altar. Take the summer indoors and decorate your home with flowers and plants. July is a time of happiness; again, if you are not then ask yourself why and take steps to help this happen, asking the Goddess for guidance. Many people struggle with being happy. They feel guilty and think they must be a rock for others, but if you're miserable you only make others miserable. Happiness is not a place we get to and then spend the rest of our life there; it's an ongoing journey of being comfortable with constant change, being confident within yourself and being pleased with who you are and who you are becoming. We cannot stop change, life is constantly changing, but we can embrace change and create our own futures rather than let future create us. The colours of this full moon are greens, silvers and greys. Adorn your altar with lemons, hyssop and chamomile. Use moonstone, opals and malachite for healing.

August - Red Moon Ψ Grain Moon Ψ Sturgeon Moon Ψ Green Corn Moon Ψ Wyrt Moon

August moon is a time of great ambition and crafts. It is also the start of the journey towards autumn; notice the days starting to get shorter. This is a time to reap rewards from your past magic work. If you have had luck from any spell working in past Esbats this is a time to thank the God and the Goddess and meditate at your altar. It is a good time for spells that work with ambition and career or money matters. Take on new projects and hobbies that interest you, look at your career and ask the Goddess to guide you and help you. Colours of this full moon are yellows, reds and oranges. Adorn your altar with basil, catnip and rosemary. Use tiger's eye, carnelian and topaz for healing.

September - Harvest Moon Ψ Corn Moon Ψ Barley Moon

September's full moon is about harvesting; not just the crops that nature has given us to eat, but also our emotions. We have travelled through summer and hopefully enjoyed it, and now it's time to give thanks and prepare for the long autumn and winter. The harvest full moon is a great time to make corn dollies. You can make these yourself or buy them online or in new age stores. Put your corn dolly on your altar and keep her throughout your home all winter to bring luck and abundance. Adorn your altar with corn, barley, wheat or any other crops which have been harvested to show thanks for these. Meditate at your altar on the full moon and thank the Goddess for her love and harvest. Thank the Sun God for his tireless work over the summer and ask both Goddess and God to watch over you through the coming dark cold nights. The colours of this full moon are browns, oranges and greens. Adorn your altar with wheat, witch hazel and flax seeds. Use citrine, peridot and bloodstone for healing.

October - Hunter's Moon Ψ Blood Moon Ψ Travel Moon Ψ Dying Grass Moon Ψ Fallen Leaf Moon

October's full moon occurs just before Samhain. Called the Hunter's Moon, it is usually very bright and our ancestors would have used this light to go hunting for meat to stock over winter. It was also a time when farmers would slaughter cattle in the harvest of flesh and so received the name Blood Moon. You should feel a big shift in energy with the changing of the seasons now, as the leaves will be falling from the trees and the air will be crisp and cold. As with Samhain, this is a time when the veil between the spirit and the living world is at its thinnest. If you have an ancestor or someone who has died that you would like to remember, place a picture of them on your altar, light a white candle to honour them and ask they join you in your Esbat. Add falling leaves and acorns to represent the season, alongside pumpkins, apples and other seasonal fruits and vegetables. This is a brilliant time for any kind of divination working, and for asking the Goddess to watch over people who have passed over. The colours of this full moon are dark blue, black and purple. Adorn your altar with apple blossom, roses, sage, rosemary and mint. Use amethyst and onyx for healing.

November - Frost Moon Ψ Beaver Moon Ψ Snow Moon

November's full moon is a time for protection; there is a long cold winter ahead and you must make sure you feel secure and warm. During this full moon we ask the Goddess to send her protection to us and our family. This is a great time to do any magical workings that will bring extra income or help you may be seeking. Use the energy of this moon to grow psychologically and meditate to understand what needs to be done to enrich your life. Heed your dreams as this is the time the earth mother will rest, as animals start to hibernate and vegetation retreats into the underworld until next spring. You should put offerings on your altar that represent the month and the season, such as fallen leaves, nuts, fruits, twigs and branches, to bring their energies towards you. The colours of this full moon are blues, brown, yellows and greys. Adorn your altar with fallen branches, fallen leaves, cayenne pepper and dill. Use jade and garnet for healing.

December - Oak Moon Ψ Cold Moon Ψ Yule Moon Ψ Long Nights Moon

The December full moon is the last full moon of the year and comes shortly after Yule, the winter solstice and longest night of the year. We welcome back the sun as the days slowly become longer and the nights shorter. This is the perfect time to reflect on the past year; ask yourself, did you do all that you could to make your life better? Did you grow spiritually? It is also a time of new beginnings so plan what you want to achieve in the year ahead and ask the Goddess to help you achieve your goals. Adorn your altar with winter fare such as holly sprigs and berries, mistletoe, nuts, fruit, evergreen branches and all the things you can find to bring the season's energies to your altar. Drink mulled wine or orange juice and rejoice for the earth coming back to life. Colours of this full moon are whites, greens, reds, golds and silvers. Adorn your altar with parsley, rosemary, sage and lemongrass. Use amazonite, apache tear and moonstone for healing.

"The word Witch carries so many negative connotations that many people wonder why we use the word at all. Yet to reclaim the word Witch is to reclaim our right, as women, to be powerful; as men, to know the feminine within as divine."

Starhawk

Covens

If you wish to practice your faith with other people you can join a coven, or alternatively you could create your own. When more than two people practice their faith together on regular days then they are entitled to class themselves as a coven. And anyone can set up a coven if they wish to.

Traditionally a coven is a group that teaches Wicca in a uniformed way, usually from teachings passed down from generations. These teachings will generally be Gardnerian, Alexandrian, Dianic or Seax. Covens often limit the number of people allowed to join and although this can vary from coven to coven this limit will usually be between nine and thirteen members. Covens are very close knit groups and to join one you would need to be initiated through some kind of initiation ceremony.

In traditional covens there will be a hierarchy; a High Priestess and a High Priest who lead all rituals. Covens meet on holy days such as the eight Sabbat solar holidays and on the Esbats of the full moons throughout the year. Rituals differ from coven to coven depending on their particular faith and the individual practices of each priest and priestess. Coven members work their way up in ranks, depending on how much they have learned. These are called degrees, with the first step being a 'first degree witch' and so on. When joining a Gardnerian or Alexandrian Coven you will be asked to sign an oath to keep all the secrets within that coven. Each coven keeps its own Book of Shadows which will traditionally be in some kind of ciphered text so others cannot read or steal their secrets.

Nowadays there are numerous 'covens' that are more open and will let anyone join who wishes to, although these are perhaps more groups than covens. However, they still practice rituals together and may even have a High Priest and High Priestess, though this is not a pre-requisite, as it is for a coven. And a coven need not be highly regimented and formal. It can just be a few friends who meet on Sabbats and Esbats and wish to practice their faith together, who sit and meditate or do spell work and rituals together for moral support.

The positive thing about being in a coven is it is a very close group of like-minded people where you can find friendship and support and make lifelong friends. It is a safe environment for self-expression. You can talk through any problems with other members and you can learn a great deal from others. One negative aspect is that some covens can become hugely dogmatic and never change or even consider fresh views. Because covens are a hierarchy, there can be a battle of egos, and if disagreements happen it can have an adverse effect on everyone. On some occasions, as people in the coven fight for status and power, it can become the exact opposite of the spiritual purpose it was designed for.

My advice is to check what covens or groups operate in your area and see if you know somebody who attends them, so you can check if you think their group is for you. Alternatively there are often meets, events and festivals happening, so you can go along to these and ask for advice. Websites such as witchvox.com provide a comprehensive list of all meets and events. For some people, taking the first step is simply down to how they think they learn best; some prefer jumping in the deep end and joining a group straight away, while others like to study and practice on their own before dipping a toe in.

"The human race is a very, very magical race. We have a magic power of witches and wizards. We're here on this earth to unravel the mystery of this planet. The planet is asking for it."

Yoko Ono

The Altar

An altar is a flat surface such as a table, trunk or shelf that we use to honour our Gods and Goddess. We use our altars for spell work and rituals, to meditate with and to call on and give thanks to the elements.

Altars are deeply personal; this should be a place you love to come to, so fill it with things that are precious to you. It is a place we go to meditate and be at one with the divine. Your altar can be a permanent feature in your home or it can be temporary and set up each time you wish to do any spell work, ritual or meditation. You don't need to spend a lot of money on your altar. Some people think they cannot be a good Wiccan unless they have absolutely everything; a broom, a wand, a chalice, an athame, an offering bowl, rune stones, tarot cards, a sword, God and Goddess statues, incense, all the coloured candles and anything else you can think of. But your altar is your own sacred space; it does not need to be like anyone else's. It may consist of just a single candle and a few seasonal leaves and a twig. A lot of people may not have room for an altar or it may not be appropriate in the household they live in. Remember the magic comes from inside you; the objects on our altars are tools to help us, they are not essential. Witchcraft and magic is inside you, so don't worry if your altar is not as extravagant as anyone else's. After time you'll start to gather and have your own personal things that mean something to you. To worship the divine you can simply look at the sky and give thanks.

Altar tools do help us in ritual and spell workings though. A typical altar will have the elements in each quarter. Fire will be on the south quarter of your altar. To represent fire have a lit candle, any colour but traditionally white. Earth will be in the north quarter of your altar. To represent earth use a little bowl of rock salt or acorns, a tree branch, crystal, stone or anything that for you represents the earth. Air will be in the east quarter of your altar, represented by burning incense or feathers. Water is in the west, represented by a goblet, a cup or chalice of water, or some sea salt.

Other tools on a typical altar would be:

Athame

An athame is a ritual knife or dagger, situated in the east quarter of your altar as it represents air. Athame's don't need to be metal; you get them made from wood or carved stone, but they would typically have a black handle. You don't actually use the athame for cutting anything in the physical world though; the athame is used for metaphysically cutting things, such as in spell work and ritual. They are used in the casting of a protective circle or cutting energies, bonds or ties.

Bell

Bells are used to draw the attentions of the divine to you and you to the divine. You can also use the bell to signify the start and end of a ritual. Bells are also useful if any unwanted energies come to you. When you are at your altar a good chime on the bell will disperse the unwanted energy.

Boline

A boline knife is used to cut herbs and other materials in spell workings. Traditionally with a white handle, many of them have a crescent moon blade, but any knife with a white handle will suffice. The athame is used for cutting spiritual energy and for circle casting, but the boline is used to cut herbs, ribbons, cords, paper and carving symbols. It sits in the south quarter of your altar.

Broomstick (Bessom)

A broomstick is made with a wooden handle and has bristles, traditionally made from heather, used to sweep away any stale or negative energy from your altar. You should sweep around your altar in a clockwise motion saying, "I sweep this place negative energy away, only the positive and love may stay."

Candles

You can have as many candles on your altar as you wish. When doing candle magic each colour signifies different outcomes, so it is always useful to keep a good supply of different coloured candles handy. For more information see the chapter on colours and candle magic on page 110.

Chalice

The chalice is a Goddess symbol and can be filled with water for your west quarter or filled with wine for certain ritualistic workings.

Cauldron

Cauldrons are usually cast iron, quite small and with three legs. Real cooking of herbal medicines or potions is done in a pot on the stove, but cauldrons are used to heat oils or for smaller spell workings such as burning of paper or photographs that are then dropped into the cauldron. If the cauldron needs to be heated you can use a tea light candle placed underneath it.

God and Goddess

To represent the God and Goddess we place two candles in the centre of our altar. The Goddess candle is white and placed on the left hand side, while the God candle is black and placed on the right hand side. A pentacle is placed in the centre, in-between the two candles. Alternatively, you can represent the God and Goddess of your choice by using statues of them.

Libation Dish

This is a small plate or bowl that sits in the centre of the altar and is used to make offerings to the God or Goddess during spell or ritual work. Offerings are given as a thank you to the deities or to keep a balance if we ask for something in our spell workings.

Offerings

Offerings to the deities could be wine, fruits, seasonal flowers, herbs, salt, bread, milk, honey, eggs or any number of other items. We give these gifts as a sign of respect and thanks to the Gods and Goddesses and to show our appreciation for anything we may receive after doing spell work. Offerings can also be representations of what we are asking for; for example if you were to do a fertility spell, you could offer an egg to the Gods.

Pentacle

A Pentacle is a five-point star encased in a circle. It is the main symbol of Wicca and brings us protection in all our workings. The pentacle can be drawn or carved into your altar or you can have it as an amulet, either placed on your altar or worn.

Wand

A wand is a magical tool made from any natural material but traditionally wood from your birth tree - see the Celtic Tree chapter on page 197. Your wand sits in the south quarter of your altar and is used to channel energy onto a certain object or towards a certain direction during spell work.

What to do at your Altar

When you go to your altar it can be for many reasons; to honour a God or Goddess and let them know you're grateful for their blessings; to meditate on a question or dilemma and ask the Gods and Goddesses for guidance, or to call the elements in performing a spell or chant. At certain times of the year, such as Sabbats and Esbats, we adorn our altars with particular items to honour the seasons or the full moons. Many people however, just do spell workings at their altar. This could be candle magic, or mixing of herbal potions, because when we call on the elements to watch over our spell casting it gives our spells strength. You can do divination at your altar as well. Many times we go to our altars just to feel the divine and the energy and to be at one with the universe.

When we go to our altars to perform spells and rituals we often cast a protective circle around ourselves so that no harm can come to us while we are at our altars. Sometimes, especially if you are working or trying to communicate with the spirit world, you will need a psychic shield of energy around you to make sure nothing can get in you don"t want to, including negative energies.

Casting a Circle

Casting a circle is to make a space of peace, a sanctuary, whilst you are at your altar. It allows you to direct your energies and create a concentrated flow of energy around you. It also keeps anything negative out, as nothing can enter the circle whilst you have it charged. To cast a circle you call on the four elements to create the circle and protect you from harm within this space of peace, balanced as it is with the power of nature.

First, take your broom and make a sweeping motion all around your altar and yourself. If you don't have a broom you can make the sweeping motion with your hands. It's done to sway air away from the area and let new air take its place.

Next, you need to ground yourself to the earth. This is accomplished through visualization. Imagine your feet are roots, let all your energy go down into the ground, feel it from the tip of your head to the tip of your toes, holding you onto and into the ground. Be at one with the ground in which you are standing. We are all made from the same energy after all; just feel it within you. A circle also creates a small space around you where you can direct your energies and create a concentrated flow of energy. After you have grounded yourself call the God and Goddess to watch over your circle casting. You can say what feels comfortable for you, and if you have a certain God or Goddess you want to call then call them in by name.

Now call the elements, starting with air in the east. Put the air element in place on your altar. If it is already on your altar then just point to it with your athame, your wand or even your finger and say, 'element of air, I call upon you to watch over me while I work' (in many parts of Wicca the different elements will have a God or a guardian and they will be called to watch over you from watchtowers, so if this is your chosen branch of Wicca call that God, Goddess or guardian to the watchtower). Next, imagine a brilliant white light coming from your wand, athame or finger, and then go onto the second element, which is fire in the south, and say, 'element of fire, I call upon you to watch over me while I work'. Then water from the west… 'element of water, I call upon you to watch over me while I work', and earth, north…'element of earth, I call upon you to watch over me while I work.' Make a circling motion and call each element to join you, and as you do this visualize a white light creating a circle of protection all around you and the altar. Now call upon the element of spirit and make the circle motion from above you to the ground and say 'as above, so below, I call upon the element of spirit', and imagine the white light creating a spherical bubble around you.

Now you have cast a circle of protection and peace in which to do either spell work or meditation at your altar. Nothing can enter or harm you while you are in this circle. You can also cast a physical circle using stones, twigs or rune stones around your altar, and this will bring strength to your circle.

When you have finished your spell work or meditation you need to close the circle, and this will be done by going in the opposite direction to casting the circle. So start with the element of spirit, and use your wand, athame or finger to cut the flowing stream of white light and say, 'I thank you element of spirit as I close the circle.' Make a cutting motion as if cutting through the white light. Now do the same with the four elements in the opposite direction you cast the circle. Thank all the elements and your God and Goddess and close the circle. Sweep away the energy either with your broom stick or with your hands.

"Energy cannot be created, nor can it be destroyed.
It can only be changed from one form to another"

Albert Einstein

Birth, Marriage and Death

Birth

In Wicca a new birth calls for a Wiccening, although in some Wiccan traditions it is called a Naming Ceremony or a Quickening. It is the event of giving a new born child a name. This is performed on the first full moon after the child's birth, and consists of presenting the child to the Goddess and asking her to look over the child throughout its life. People who come to a Wiccening ceremony are asked to bring something symbolic of the child's astrology sign, such as a gemstone, or a toy or clothing of that astrological colour. The people then present their gift to the child in turn, and either say a poem or ask the Goddess to present the child with certain gifts to help throughout life. These are like wishes, and should be written in a book for the child to see when they become old enough.

You set up an altar and light a candle that corresponds to the astrological sign of the child. Cast a circle around the altar with the mother and child in the centre, then invite each guest to come unto the child, give their gift and write down the wish they have for the child. If you are in a coven this will be done by the coven members, or if you wish you can contact a High Priest or Priestess and ask them to perform the ceremony in the tradition you follow.

Marriage (Handfasting)

When Wiccans marry it is called a handfasting. This is a temporary or permanent marriage, consecrated by the tying of a ribbon around the joined hands of the couple. It can last for one year and one day or it can be a permanent marriage. These marriages can be legal; you just swap the tying of a ribbon around hands for the exchanging of rings in a civil ceremony, or you can do rings and the ribbon if you wish. However, if the marriage is a temporary one held by a High Priestess it will probably not be seen as a legal contract. A handfasting can be done with same sex couples as well as with a man and women, and in many states and countries same sex marriage is now legally recognised by law.

Death

Wiccans do not fear death. Of course we are sorry to see a loved one die and we will miss them terribly, but we know that we will see them again. Remember The Great Wheel: 'what has been will be again.' Death is a transition, not an end. Everything in the universe is and always will be, nothing new is ever made and nothing ever dies, energy just transforms into other matter and forms. We believe that everything has a cycle. A plant starts from seed and is grown, it then blossoms and seeds and eventually dies and is turned into compost to feed the next generation of plants. A rock is made from magma from the centre of the earth, it cools down and with time, with waves and weather is then crushed down to dust or sand.

The universe, in its ever expanding state, turns dense dark matter and gasses into a star which becomes bright and burns for millions of years but eventually explodes in a supernova, without which there would be no oxygen or carbon or any of the life-giving gasses or elements that we need to live. Humans are made from seed and are born, change, and then eventually die, and our energy transforms to become part of the universe as it was before. Ultimately the universe is expanding and has been since the big bang and it will eventually implode in on itself and then the whole process will start all over again. This has and always will keep happening forever.

We are like a drop of rain falling into the ocean, only to be eventually taken back up into the clouds, to be a drop of rain again falling back into the ocean.

People from different pantheons in Wicca will have their own pantheon's idea of death. If you are of the ancient Egyptians faith then you will believe you are shepherded into the next world by Anubis or Osiris, to be judged by Thoth in a weighing of the heart ceremony, and if your heart weighs less than an ostrich feather you will be granted passage to a paradise. In Norse Pantheon you will go with Odin to Valhalla if you lived a strong warrior's life and fought for good and justice, and if you lived a happy and just life you would go with Freya in Folkvangr. But if you did not do anything positive with your life or were bad you will go to the Goddess Hel. In the Celtic pantheon, The Morrigan is often seen at death and will carry you away to the otherworld, especially if you die in battle or fighting for truth and justice. Rhiannon is another Goddess of the otherworld who shepherds the dead on her white horse. In the Greek and Roman Pantheon meanwhile, there are many Gods and Goddesses of death and the underworld.

The Summerlands

Many Wiccans believe in a place called the Summerlands. This is a place we go to when we die, akin to a waiting room for your spirit, which can then contemplate on life and watch over earth and loved ones. It is a place where we wait to be transformed into other energies in the universe. In Wicca there isn't a wall between life and death; it is more of a vial, where we can still contact the spirit of people who have moved into the Summerlands. This vial is at its thinnest between the hours of midnight and 3am, known as 'The Witching Hour', and it becomes thinner again at Samhain and Beltane.

A Wiccan Funeral

Most Wiccans are not that interested in their bodies once they die, as their spirit has left the vessel it was using while on the earth plane. And so some Wiccans do not mind if non Wiccan family or friends wish to give them a Christian, Muslim or Jewish funeral, as this funeral is more for the living than the dead. If it gives your friends and family peace and a closure then this is fine. Your Wiccan friends or coven may hold their own private funeral ceremony when you pass.

Wiccans just want their body to be put back into the earth, either by burial or by cremation and their ashes being scattered. It is perfectly legal in most countries to have a pentagram placed on your headstone if you so wish. Many pagans in the military have this done. You can ask your coven (if you belong to one) to carry out any funeral wishes, which will have to be signed in the presence of a lawyer, if you want your Wiccan funeral conducted by the High Priest and Priestess. You can also choose to have a humanist burial, which isn't a religious burial at all but more a celebration of the life of the person.

"Anytime you feel love for anything, be it stone, tree, lover, or child, you are touched by the Goddess's magick..."

Cate Tiernan

The Book of Shadows

A Book of Shadows is a Wiccan journal that you write in to record all the work you do regarding your Wicca path. You should write down everything you have learned, so it becomes a reference book or your own personal bible if you like.

Here's some things to write down:

Dreams

Ritual work

Spells

Potions

Herbs

Candle magic

Elements Workings

Poetry

Chants

Prayers

Any Gods or Goddesses you feel close to.

Write down anything regarding your spiritual Wiccan journey, your emotions, how certain spells or rituals made you feel and any new knowledge learnt so it can be referred to at a later date.

The book can be as elaborate or as simple as you want it to be. You can buy expensive ones online or from a metaphysical store, or you can just use a normal jotter and decorate it in your own way. But it does need to be something with a lot of pages that will stand the test of time. You may make as many Books of Shadows as you like and throughout a lifetime you will probably get through quite a few books. You could even have different books; one for spells, one for potions, a personal dream directory etc. It may be helpful if you make an index in the book so it will be easy to find what you are looking for. You can keep recipes and cut outs of materials you like to use, or keep dried flowers, herbs and leaves in some chapters to help you remember.

Covens keep a group Book of Shadows with the rites and rituals that the coven uses. Many are particularly secretive about their spells and ritual workings and sometimes the Book of Shadows will be in code or a cipher so nobody can read it except for initiated members of the coven.

The Witches Alphabet

ꝿ	A	ʊ	I	ꝗ	Q
ꝗ	B	ʊ	J	ꝳ	R
ꝿ	C	ꝿ	K	ꝿ	S
ꝿ	D	ꝿ	L	ꝿ	T
ꝿ	E	ꝿ	M	ꝿ	U
ꝿ	F	ꝿ	N	ꝿ	V
ꝿ	G	ꝿ	O	ꝿ	W
ꝿ	H	ꝿ	P	ꝿ	X
				ꝿ	Y
				ꝿ	Z

The Witches Alphabet or Theban Alphabet as it is also known is an ancient alphabet with origins that are lost in the mists of time. Often called "The Runes of Honorius" after its reputed inventor, Honorius of Thebes, the first printed version can be traced back to 1518 when it was published by an occultist called Johannes Trithemius. Many Witches use this alphabet to write when they want to keep their spells secret. You can also use the letters of the alphabet in your spell work, to write the name of someone or something you want. It's also said witches used the alphabet to communicate with each other in secret.

You can make talismans or sigils by combining the letters to make pictures. For example, if you desired luck you would take the Theban letters L U C K and fashion them into a joined symbol to bring you luck. So it makes a sigil like the image below:

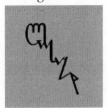

The letters are said to have magical properties and through time have become known as the Witches Alphabet. Numerous covens use this alphabet for their book of shadows so their secrets cannot be stolen by the unlearned. You can also use the symbols of rune stones to make magical sigils.

"For every action there is an equal and opposite reaction"

Sir Isaac Newton

Morals and Codes

Wiccans have numerous morals and codes they live by, all circled by the laws of nature and the universe, by our own sense of balance and the universal balance.

Wiccans believe in Karma, although Karma is not exclusively a Wiccan thing as it features heavily in Buddhism, Hinduism and Sikhism. When someone throws a stone into a pool of water, the ripples flow outwards, but when they reach the sides of the pool they start to make their way back to the exact point where the stone hit the water in the first place. Remember the importance of balance; if you do something it will eventually end up coming back to you. Some Wiccans, including those in the Gardnerian tradition, believe what you send out into the universe comes back to you threefold. This Law of Three is in the Wiccan Rede, a guide to living used in covens for hundreds of years, though not every Wiccan follows the Wiccan Rede.

A moral system or code said as a poem, it is a mystery as to where the Rede originates. Many Wiccans simply live by the statement, "Eight words the Wiccan Rede fulfil - An it harm none, do as ye will," meaning as long as what you do doesn't hurt anyone, do what you want.

The Wiccan Rede

Bide the Wiccan law ye must
In perfect love and perfect trust
Live ye must and let to live
Fairly take and fairly give
True in love, ever be
Lest thy love be false to thee

With a fool no season spend
Nor be counted as his friend
Soft of eye and light of touch
Speak ye little, listen much

Ever mind the rule of three
What ye send out comes back to thee
This lesson well, thou must learn
Ye only get what ye do earn

Eight words the Wiccan Rede fulfil
'An it harm none, do as ye will'

Deosil go by waxing Moon
Sing and dance the invoking Rune
Widdershins go by waning Moon
Chant ye then a freeing tune

When the Lady's Moon is new
Kiss thy hand to Her times two
When the Bow rides in the eve
Turn to what you would achieve
When the Moon rides at her peak
Then thy heart's desire seek
When the Sickle shows Her face
Release the old with proper grace

Greet the Days and greet the Nights
With joy and thanks for all delights
Sing the seasons all around
Til wondrous awe and love abound

Heed the North Wind's mighty gale
Lock the door & trim the sail

When the wind comes from the South
Love will kiss thee on the mouth

When the wind blows from the West
Hearts will find their peace and rest
When the wind blows from the East
Expect the new and set the feast

Nine woods in the Cauldron go
Burn them quick and burn them slow
Birch and fir and apple tree
Hawthorn is sacred to Thee
Willow, hazel, rowan, grape
And oak will shape the weave of fate
Elder be the Lady's tree
Burn it not or cursed ye
Birchwood in the fire goes
To tell us true what Goddess knows
Oak trees tower great with might
Burn the Oak for God's insight
Rowan is a tree of power
Causing life and magic to flower
Willows at the waters stand
To help us to the Summerland
Hawthorn burn to purify
And draw the faerie to your eye
Hazel tree, the wisdom sage
Lends strength that comes with honoured age
White the flowers of Apple tree
The holy gift of fecundity
Grape grows upon the fruitful vine
Sacred gifts of joy and wine
Fir's ever greenness declares life
Succeeds beyond any strife

82

Heed ye flower, bush, and tree
And by the Lady Blessed be
Where the rippling waters flow
Cast a stone and truth ye'll know

Four times the Major Sabbats mark
In the light and in the dark

As the old year starts to wane
The new begins with dark Samhain
When flowers blossom through the snow
Fair Brighid casts her seed to sow
When winter yields to warmth's return
Let the Beltane fires burn
As summer turns to Lammas night
First fruits and Grain Gods reach their height

Four times the Minor Sabbats fall
Use the Sun to mark them all

At Yuletide, with feast and mirth
We celebrate the God Child's birth
Spring Equinox, Eostara's fest
All newborn creatures will be blessed
When the Sun has reached its height
Celebrate the greatest Light
Offer thanks at second reaping
Mabon poised for winter's sleeping

Cast the circle thrice about
To keep unwelcome spirits out
To bind the spell well every time
Let the spell be spake in rhyme

Follow this with mind & art
Bright the cheeks and warm the heart
And merry meet & merry part
And merry meet again

Free Will

Do not mess around with others free will; this is wrong to do. When we do spell work we should not do the spells on other people to make them do something they wouldn't normally do, at least not without their permission. If it was the other way round and somebody made you do things you didn't want to I'm sure you wouldn't be happy. If someone asks you to create a spell for them or put a spell on them then that is fine, as long as it harms nobody of course, but you shouldn't do spells on anyone unwittingly. Here's an important example: doing a spell to attract love or make you irresistible is fine, but to put a spell on a certain individual to make them love you is wrong. It will not turn out well and the person will not really love you. There are certain times you can put spells on people as long as it doesn't impede on their free will; if someone is lost or missing then it's perfectly fine to do a spell to help find them. In general, it is fine to do spell work on people as long as you leave their free will intact.

In Wicca we act according to the law, 'Harm None, But Do as Ye Will.' This means you can virtually do whatever you like as long as it causes no harm. The Harm None rule doesn't mean you should let people walk all over you or you should never fight back. If you let harm come to you or your family then in effect you're breaking the rule by letting harm come to yourself or others. The Harm None rule works across the board; as Wiccans it is our duty to step in if we see harm or anyone being harmed. Bear in mind Karma, remember the balance and you cannot go wrong.

"And above all, watch with glittering eyes the whole world around you because the greatest secrets are always hidden in the most unlikely places. Those who don't believe in magic will never find it"

Roald Dahl

"Ultimately, the purpose of magic is to free our potential, not bind us to ideas"

Philip Carr-Gomm

How to do Magic

Magic is not dangerous, evil or scary. Some people like to place a mystique around magic to make it seem much more fantastical than it really is. But magic is all around us; every time the suns rises; every time a mighty tree grows from an acorn; every time we put our will on something and make it happen; every time a baby is born. Every day of our lives is magical. Don't be scared of magic; experiment with it, feel the power of nature, learn about herbs, stones, crystals and combining the elements. Most of all believe in the power that is within you; your words have power, your thoughts have power, your actions have power, colours have power and symbols have power. Magic is nature and nature is you. Don't fear magic - embrace it. Medicine is magic, a mix of ingredients to have an effect upon a person, a potion. Science is basically the understanding of the natural world; this is magic too. The word 'scientist' did not exist until the 1830's. Before that, they were referred to as 'natural philosophers.' Witches, druids and shaman were the pioneers of science, astrology and medicine.

Magic is all part of our connection to nature and the universe. Wiccans believe everything is connected to everything else. We are made from 90% of the same things that stars are made of, with the exception of hydrogen and helium. We are the universe in human form, with universal amounts of power inside each one of us. The five elements create all that life needs to thrive. As the sun gives us warmth and crops, so we tend and eat these crops. Wildlife lives on the flora of the land and keep it sustained and balanced. The moon controls the tides and oceans and works in harmony with the sun, both being exactly the perfect distance from each other.

There is a saying in magic, "what is above, so is below." This means that everything is connected to everything else, that the universe is the same as the Gods and Goddesses, who are the same as man, who is the same as the cell, which is the same as the atom, which is the same as a neutron and so on, ad infinitum. The fact everything is connected is not just a Wiccan view but is also held by modern science and quantum physics. We are all connected to each other biologically, to the earth chemically and to the universe atomically.

That connection is how we do our magical workings; we use this connection to tap into and try to will change. Magic doesn't just work by lighting a certain coloured candle and burning some incense and saying a few enchanted words. To create magic it must come from your will and your intent. In fact, the vast majority of magic works on will alone. When you create a spell or say a chant or incantation you must feel it with every part of your being. Magic is not easy and can be very draining. It can also take a lot of practice to get into the right frame of mind. The best way to learn is through meditation; you need to tap into your subconscious mind as this is where most of the real magic happens. Our minds are so filled with day to day tasks and issues such as work, family, money, bills and chores it can be really difficult to shut our mind off and perform magic at our best. Through meditation you can learn to shut all these out and open your third eye, your magic eye.

A great deal of magic involves using tools such as wands, herbs, candles, chanting, or drawing symbols we call sigils. Magic comes in many forms but remember the magic comes from within you, from your actions and your own will.

There are four rules when it comes to magic:

Rule 1
Don't mess with others free will.

Rule 2
Harm none, do as you will

Rule 3
Don't be greedy; the universe and everything in it is about keeping a balance.

Rule 4
Stay within the law.

If you ask for too much when you do magic you are tipping the balance and going against the laws of nature. If you are struggling with money then it's fine to ask for help in paying your bills and you could ask for new clothes or shoes, but if you ask to win the lottery through magic this is a major tipping of the balance and bad luck may well befall you. There is a story I always tell as an example of this. There was a young witch who was sick of having no money and so she cast a spell to be rich. A few days went by and she was as poor as ever. Then one morning she had a knock at the door. It was the police who told her that her parents had died in a house fire the previous night. Obviously, she was terribly upset. Then later that day a solicitor came to the door and told her she had inherited a fortune from her parents' life insurance. The young witch remembered the spell and was so full of guilt and grief she gave all the money away to a charity, and was left still penniless but now without parents.

When we do any kind of magic we must always try to keep a balance. Whatever you ask for doesn't materialize out of nowhere; it must come from somewhere. Sometimes if we do ask for a big thing a sacrifice may be needed to balance things out. This could be a money sacrifice given to a charity of your choice. A favourite food you have could be placed on your altar as a sacrifice to the Gods. We do not sacrifice living things; it is against the law and frowned upon by Wiccans.

And as for Rule 4, staying within the law; media and modern mainstream religions have helped foster and maintain negative images of pagan worship. Don't fuel their fears and discriminations; help us allay them. In today's society, magic can sometimes appear to be a bit 'on the edge.' Certain spells call for you to be skyclad, meaning naked. This is fine in your own house but is not fine in a public park. Just keep the law in mind when performing any magic.

Time to do Magic

There are specific times to do magic or ask for things to come into or leave our lives, such as certain days of the week or certain moon phases. The moon is our Goddess; we worship it and do our magic with it.

New Moon

This is when the new moon is dark. The mysterious crone aspect of the Triple Moon Goddess, it is a time for new beginnings, the best time to start any spell workings or a new aspect of our lives, such as getting a new job, or starting a new hobby or skill. It is a time to let go of the past and start afresh, bringing something new into our lives. Let go of anything that is holding you back or weighing you down with negativity. Ask yourself what you need to grow. Life is all about change; the world changes, people change, you change, everything changes whether you like it or not. You cannot stay in the same mind-set you were in years before; you have to grow and change and how you do this is up to you. You can take positive steps and change for the better or you can be bogged down with negativity and get stuck in a circle of misfortune. On the new moon we ask ourselves what it is we need to do for change and for taking our lives in a positive direction, and we use the moon phases to help us achieve this.

Waxing Moon

The waxing moon starts immediately after the new moon, with the Goddess in her maiden aspect. This is a time for spell working to bring positive things to us, such as our improvements to our love lives, our working lives, our finances or spiritual lives. Ask yourself what you can do to bring balance, harmony and peace within yourself. Take steps to make positive changes. Use the waxing moon for learning something new, taking up a new hobby or interest, starting a new project, perhaps something you have been putting off for a while. Take chances and risks, surprise yourself and impress yourself. Allow yourself to be happy.

Full Moon

In Wicca we call the full moon an Esbat. This is when the Goddess is now in her mother aspect. It is a time to soak up the psychic energy of the full moon and honour the Goddess. It is a time of full circles. Put into fruition the things you started on the new moon. It is a time of thanks and for being grateful for what we have. No matter how little you have, always be grateful, for gratitude attracts good things to you. If you are not grateful for what you already have then having more of it will not make you happy. Use the energy of the full moon to bring plans into action, to bring about positive change and energy to your life. This is a wonderful time to do divinisation such as tarot reading and rune casting. It is also a time of contemplation and deep thought, so meditate on questions you have and seek answers.

Waning Moon

The waning moon comes after the full moon and will continue waning until it is a new moon once more. The waning moon is a time to expel anything we no longer want in our lives. The Goddess is in her wise crone aspect, has learned life's lessons and is putting them to use. If there is anything you feel is holding you back or stopping you from growing then use this moon phase to get rid of it. Cut anything out of your life that is making you unhappy. This is a good time for spiritual cleansing and releasing yourself from negativity. Let go of the past, let go of past hurts and learn to forgive people who have wronged you. You don't need to forgive for the other person; forgive for your own sense of peace, because when we forgive we stop people from having power over us. Holding onto hurt and pain means hurting yourself more than anybody else. This is a good time to smudge your home to get rid of negativity and stale energy. To learn about smudging see the Rituals and Spells chapter on page 153.

The days of the week are also relevant for the best times to do magic, rituals or spell working, or to bring about change.

Monday

Monday is the day named after the Moon Gods and Goddesses. The colours of Monday are silvers and whites. The herbs associated with Monday are sage, mint, white roses and willow. Monday is a good time for creativity and wisdom, a good time for new starts and seeking answers to truths.

Tuesday

Tuesday is named after the God Tyr. Other Gods associated with Tuesday are Mars, Ares and The Morrighan. The colours of Tuesday are red and orange. The herbs associated with Tuesday are cactus, thistles, nettles and holly. Tuesday is about conflicts and settling old scores. This is a good day to dispel anyone who brings negativity into your life.

Wednesday

Wednesday is named after the God Woden (Odin). Other Gods associated with this day are Lugh, Hermes, Mercury and Athena. The colour of Wednesday is purple. Herbs associated are lavender, lilies, honeysuckle, aspen trees and ferns. Wednesday is about finance, business and pulling together your resources. It is also about creativity and arts such as painting, crafts and poetry.

Thursday

Thursday is named after the God Thor. Other gods associated with Thursday are Zeus, Jupiter and Juno. The colours of Thursday are blue and green. Herbs associated are oak trees, basil, rosemary and lemongrass. Thursday is a day of strength and power, to look inwards to your own strengths. It is a magical day when it is good to do almost all spells.

Friday

Friday is named after Goddess Frigg or Freya. Other Gods associated with this day are Venus and Aphrodite. Fridays are associated with pink and light red colours. Herbs associated with Friday are red berries, roses, blossoms, apples and peaches. Friday is a day of love, a time to work on relationships and friendships.

Saturday

Saturday is named after the God Saturn. Other Gods associated with this day are Hecate. The colour of Saturday is black and blood red. Herbs associated with Saturday are thyme, cumin, cloves and dill. Saturday is a day of protection spells and banishment spells. It is the best time to rid negativity and to protect yourself and your home.

Sunday

Sunday is named after the sun and the Sun Gods and Goddesses. The colours of Sunday are yellow and gold. Herbs associated are cinnamon, sunflowers, salt, marigolds, garlic, ginger, nutmeg and juniper berries. Sunday is a day of peace, a day of creativity, self-expression and victories. The best spells are ones of ambitious plans, of healing and growing.

Visualisation

Visualisation is a magical tool to put you into the right frame of mind for spell work. It is the method of visualising what you want. When we do this we don't just have a picture of what we are wishing for in our head. You have to want it more than you have ever wanted anything. Don't simply see the thing you are visualising in your mind's eye; manifest it, feel it, smell it, touch it, imagine having it. Plant it into your subconscious. By doing this you are sending a clear message to the universe, as thoughts are energy and anything that has energy is manifested into the universe.

To use visualisation, sit comfortably in a place you will not be disturbed, get a bowl of water and light a candle so the flames reflection can be seen in the water. Now stare at the flame in the bowl and visualise what it is that you want to manifest. Keep doing this for as long as you wish, from ten minutes to an hour or even longer. Write the thing you were visualising on a piece of paper and draw a pentagram underneath. Now burn the paper on the candle flame and drop it into the water. Take the water and throw it into the earth with the ashes of the paper. Look up at the stars and the moon and give thanks.

Another way to visualise is to meditate. Sit comfortably, close your eyes, visualise what you want to manifest in your mind and try to solely concentrate on this thing. Let everything else disappear and your mind become blank of all other thoughts. You can do this for as long as you wish…

Meditation

Meditation is a wonderful way to centre and balance yourself. We often have so much stress and worry in day to day life that we need a place of calm and solitude so we can gather our thoughts and relax our mind, spirit and body. Meditation is especially good if you need to know an answer to a question or problem. If you meditate on it for long enough the solution should come to you. Meditation is tapping into your subconscious mind, which is where magic happens. In scientific studies they have discovered that the subconscious mind is ten thousand times more powerful than the conscious mind. Your subconscious mind holds and sorts through millions of bits of data every second. It keeps your heart beating and keeps you breathing without you even thinking about it. Essentially it keeps you alive. Meditation has been used for thousands of years by many civilizations and is a way to tap into your subconscious mind and attain a higher state of consciousness at one with the universe and the divine. Indeed science has proven that the body normally vibrates at G sharp, but in meditation it rises to A, a semi-tone higher. There are many forms of meditation and if you need more assistance there are some excellent books, videos and websites that can give you further information and depth on them.

Listed below are some simple meditation techniques to get you started.

Basic Meditation

Find yourself a nice, comfortable and quiet place to sit or lie down. Close your eyes and relax for a few minutes. Let all the muscles in your body go limp, clear all thoughts from your mind, let go of worry and stress and turn your thoughts inward. Go deep inside yourself, into the darkness of your subconscious, and let your subconscious take over all thought and feeling until you feel you are not even present anymore, you're just energy. Be at one with everything. Like everything else, meditation needs practice. At first it may be difficult to give yourself up to your subconscious mind as it's usually something we do only when we are sleeping. But practice can make perfect and you will get better and better at it the more you try.

Breathing Meditation

Sit or lie in a comfortable position in a place you will not be disturbed and close your eyes. Let yourself become relaxed, allow your muscles to become weak and limp and clear your mind of all thoughts. Now listen to your breathing; don't change it, just listen for a few minutes. Start to control your breaths. Inhale deeply and exhale all the way out. Do this for a few minutes and then let your breathing go back to its normal rhythm for a few minutes. Again, take deep breaths, inhaling as far as you can and exhaling as far as you can for a few minutes. Keep doing this for as long as you need to whilst letting your mind go to another place. In fact, let it control you and take you wherever it wants to go. Some people find it easier to cover their ears while doing this technique as it makes the breaths louder and therefore helps them to concentrate.

Mantra

Mantra is the technique of saying a sound, word or even a sentence over and over again, a common practice in Hinduism with the word Om, where the sound of the word relates to the vibration of the universe and is a way to align your body's vibration alongside it. Sit or lie in a comfortable position in a place you will not be disturbed, let your muscles and your body relax totally and when you feel relaxed say Ommmmmmmmmmmmmmm for as long as your breath will hold out. Then take a deep breath and say it again and repeat. You don't have to say Om. There are many different mantras you can say or sounds you can make; it's up to you how you choose to do it. You can repeat words you wish to accomplish, such 'I will get this promotion.'

92

Sound Meditation

Sound meditation is a technique where you play sounds to meditate by, usually natural sounds such as birdsong, waves or even a thunderstorm, though it could also be mediation music. These sounds can easily be found online on websites such as You Tube. Again, find a comfortable spot to sit or lie down where you will not be disturbed. Play the sound that you wish to mediate to. Listen to it, let your muscles and body relax and clear your mind of everything but the sounds, then let these sounds transport you and take you to where your mind wants to go.

"Dreams pass into the reality of action. From the actions stems the dream again; and this interdependence produces the highest form of living"

Anais Nin

How to Interpret your Dreams

Don't be fooled by those books or websites that state they can interpret your dreams through signs and symbols such as a dream dictionary. This is impossible. Symbols and signs are unique to each of us. If you are afraid of spiders and dream of them, than that may be a bad omen, but if you adore spiders and keep them as pets then the dream obviously means something totally different. If you were afraid of flying and dreamed about aeroplanes it could be unpleasant, but if you love aeroplanes and even went skydiving then again, this would have a very different meaning.

Dreams are personal and symbols can mean something to one person and something totally different to someone else. The best way to interpret a dream is to dissect it, take it bit by bit and analyse what it can mean in your own life. Dreams are your way, while unconscious, to work out something in your life. They may even be able to forewarn of a bad thing that is going to happen, as examples of this have happened time and time again throughout history.

As an example; if you were to dream about a scorpion and you are terrified of scorpions think what this might mean to you. Figure out what or who the scorpion represents and where you were in the dream when you saw it. If you were in a house from your childhood the scorpion may represent a person you disliked or an event that happened in the past. It may indicate that you are worried about seeing this person once more or this event happening again. Has a person shown up again in your life that you do not like?

If you keep dreaming about a certain person, try to figure out why, think of where you are in your dream, what is the situation, if you're happy or scared. If you keep dreaming about a certain object, think further about that object. Where is it? How does it act? Does it move or is it distorted? What are your feelings when seeing this object? When your dreams keep putting you into a certain position then take time and think about this. Perhaps you find yourself in different and new places in your dreams, and this makes you feel vulnerable and even scared. But then something happens, or someone comes along and you're reassured and comfortable. Maybe your subconscious is telling you that you can move on in life, that you will find that better job or better person, if you have the confidence to make that move into the unknown.

Dream analysis can be very useful in helping you figure out many issues in your life. Important things to look out for and ask yourself are:

Where are you in the dream?
Who is in the dream with you?
How do you feel in the dream?
Is it a dream or a nightmare?
What animals are there?
What elements do you see…earth, fire, water, sky?
Is it day or night?

Now you need to ask yourself what these things mean in your life, what they represent. Look deeper as they may be a message you need to know. Keep a dream diary and write them down in your Book of Shadows. Look for patterns in your life and see if they relate to patterns in your dreams. Allow dreams to feed your creativity and most importantly, learn what you can from them so that you can grow as a person, do what is right and move forwards in life.

"If you want to find the secrets of the universe, think in terms of energy, frequency and vibration"

Nikola Tesla

Colour and Candle Magic

Colours can change a vibration of a place or situation and consequently can be a significant help with your magical workings. Everything that vibrates gives off waves of energy and colours are no different, vibrating at different levels depending on their hue. Red is the colour that vibrates the fastest, while purple is the slowest. You can use colour through candles, paper, ink, objects, paint and symbolism - in fact anything you can think of.

It is well known within the food industry that colours have a massive effect on us. The fast food industry uses a lot of red, a fast fiery colour that is vibrant and attracts and makes some people automatically feel hungry. Many restaurants have subtle colours and tones like beiges and browns, as these are relaxed and they want you to stay for as long as possible. Traffic lights turn red to tell us stop - you might get ran over! Blue for a baby boy and pink for a baby girl? You might not agree with this, but it's there for a reason, not a coincidence. Colours say a great deal about peoples' choice too. Some have a bright and vibrant wardrobe, others greys and blacks, some subtle but colourful. The choices we make say something about how we perceive ourselves, and how we want others to perceive us. This can be a truly individual and unique choice or part of a wider desire to see ourselves and our identity as relating to something bigger, such as a particular group or social standing.

To learn about colours and their importance within Wicca, look at nature and its glorious colours, its extraordinary vibrant arrays and patterns. In nature colours are so important they are almost a language themselves; they proclaim, I'm dangerous, I'm poisonous, I'm fertile, I'm ripe, I'm sweet, I'm sour, I'm angry and much more. Natural colours are often universal, such as the greens of vegetation, the blues of sea and sky, the reds and oranges of fires and volcanoes and the vibrant seductive colours of flowers. Markings on animals tell other animals specific messages. Every colour has its meaning and a magical significance.

Red

Red symbolises danger and for many animals the colour red signifies the animal is poisonous, or it simply means do not approach. Use reds in your magical workings as warnings or protection. Of course it is also the colour of passion, the colour someone turns when they blush, or when they become sexually aroused. Red has a great deal of energy attached to it. Use it for spells that require energy, such as keeping fit or losing weight. Use red to bring passion into your life. Use it to draw power to yourself or enhance your willpower. Red is also used in magic for ambition and moving forward with your career, and an excellent colour to draw on courage or to fight illness.

Keywords: blood, lust, passion, energy, power, will, sex, courage, attraction, survival, health and ambition.

Pink

Pink is the colour to use when you want to draw on a friendship or patch up after an argument or disagreement. It's an emotional colour so use it to do a spell that will heal a broken heart or a rift with family; many healing crystals are pink. Attract love, romance and friendship with its soft blossoms and roses. Think about its colours within nature to work with it magically.

Keywords: love, friendships, emotions, feminine, romance, caring, harmony and tenderness.

Yellow

Yellow is an intelligence colour, associated with magic of the mind. If you wish to learn more, if you want the truth or if you want to start a new learning activity such as college or university then use yellow. It's also connected to creativity so if you wish to learn a new skill or craft then do spells with yellow candles or crystals or something from nature the colour yellow. You can find yellows everywhere; from fruit to flowers, from herbs to crystals and not forgetting of course the beautiful bright yellow of the sun.

Keywords: intellect, mind, logic, thinking, knowledge, the sun, growth, creativity and communication.

Orange

Orange is an ambition colour so use it to achieve goals in love or work. It's also a colour for positivity, so if you have been feeling down or peoples' language or behaviour have left you feeling low, use orange as a positivity booster. Orange is also connected to parties and fun, energy and vitality. Find orange within nature in zest, acid, spice and fire.

Keywords: positivity, fun, energy, changes, moving forward, goal setting and happiness.

Green

Green is the colour of nature, a colour that represents growth in many different contexts, including spiritual growth, a new home, a new job or a new baby. Use it in spells for prosperity and anything you wish to grow or increase. Green is also a healing colour and draws on the healing properties of herbs and nature's natural greenery. You should use green in any kind of earth based magic or for growth, fertility, healing and prosperity.

Keywords: fertility, prosperity, money, wealth, growth, balance, nature and healing.

Blue

Blue is a colour for relaxation and tranquillity; use it in spell work for calming yourself or others. It can manifest bliss too, so use it if you want to bring a reward toward yourself for a job well done. Blue is a good colour to use for protection and when meditating and is also the colour of truth if you feel you are being deceived. Lighter blues are more calming and darker blues more psychic. Look at blues in nature, such as water, sky, flowers and crystals.

Keywords: calm, peace, tranquilly, bliss, truth, protection and meditation.

Purple

Purple is a psychic colour and is excellent for bringing a problem to the surface and to see what you previously could not. Burn purple candles when doing any form of divination, such as tarot, runes or scrying. Use when meditating and to bring luck. Think of purples in nature, in lightning, a purple sky, crystals such as amethyst, purple herbs and flowers such as lavender.

Keywords: psychic, consciousness, luck, protection, wisdom, meditation, spiritual, mysterious and unlocking truths.

Brown

Brown is an earth colour used in healing spells and brings extra power when using wood or herbs in spell work. It is a colour of strength and can be used for bringing positivity and stability within the home, family and work. Use it to draw an object to you that you feel you need; brown is the colour of soil and wood, the most life giving things on the planet. Trees give us oxygen and house millions of animals. We use wood to make houses, fires, furniture and many other things. Brown soil is the basis of life for herbs, flowers, trees and vegetation. It is the ground we walk upon.

Keywords: strength, earth, healing, stability, prosperity, home, garden, family and needed objects.

Black

Black is the colour of the unknown and the unseen, of night and shadow. It's used in magic to represent the new moon and new beginning or things we are not able to see. Use as a protector to break curses or hexes put upon us and to expel negative energies. Black is also a blank canvas, the in-between of space, full of potential energy. It can also be used to call on the power of Sun Gods because black absorbs the sun's energies better than any colour in the spectrum.

Keywords: protection, The God, reversing curses and hexes, absorption, justice, endings, power and banishing.

White

White is the colour of purity, of spirit and The Goddess. Untainted, it is pure energy, akin to a new born baby, the first fall of snow and life giving properties of milk, and so it is often used in healing and cleansing. Use white to visualize as white light can extinguish darkness and dark or unwanted entities. White is all the other colours combined; it does not have absorption, it only gives out.

Keywords: the Goddess, purity, wholeness, spirituality, healing, opening up magic, raising vibration to another level, all the other colours combined, healing light and asking for wishes.

Candle Magic

When doing candle magic, you should be in a quiet place where you can concentrate. Make sure your candle is the correct colour for what you want to achieve. Many people carve a pentacle onto the candle or a name, initials, or word to help with the spell. Make sure you concentrate fully on the spell you are doing. Hold the candle in your hands for a while and focus your energies into the candle.

Anointing a Candle

It can give the spell extra strength if we anoint the candle with the correct type of oil for that particular spell. You can make your own oil by steeping a certain herb in olive oil for ten days, something I've found works just as well as essential oil. Anointing a candle is the practise of covering the candle in the oil and then burring the candle and asking for what you wish to achieve with the spell; for example, use rose oil and pink candles to attract love. To anoint a candle, pour a little oil into one hand and then rub your palms together until your hands are covered in the oil. Think of the spells purpose while doing this. To attract things towards you start in the middle of the candle and then rub the oil upwards to the top then down to the bottom. To draw things away from you that you no longer want in your life, start at the middle of the candle and rub the oil downwards first then when you reach the base go upwards to the top. To reverse a spell do the same spell but anoint the candle in the opposite direction you did when you first performed the spell.

Dressing a Candle

Dressing a candle is when we add things to the candle to help with spell work; these can be symbols, names, patterns or shapes we inscribe in the candle to give a spell more power. You can also rub herbs or oil into the candle. You can make your own candle and add herbs or oil, or you can add a small amount of olive oil to your candle and then rub either dried or fresh herbs onto the candle so they stick to it.

The Pentagram and Pentacle

The symbol of Wicca is the pentagram, a five pointed star representing the essence of life. The five points represents the elements. The top represents spirit, the point on its right represents water, the next is fire, the next earth and the final point air. The pentagram is usually encased within a circle which makes it a pentacle, an amalgamation of the two words pentagram and circle. When it has a circle around it this makes it a sign of protection.

We use the pentacle as a symbol of faith and wear it as jewellery, a tattoo or carry a picture around of one, as it is not only a symbol of the faith but a powerful protection tool. We nearly always keep a pentagram around us, especially on our altar or when performing any spell workings.

Invoking and Banishing

We can use the pentagram in our magical workings to invoke something, bringing it to you, or to banish something, which entails sending it away from you. You do not need to physically draw the pentagram; you can draw it in the air using your wand, athame or finger. To invoke anything draw the pentagram from spirit, which is the top point, then go around the elements in order of their density so after spirit draw a line to the fire point, then a line to air, then a line to water then a line to earth, and then finish at spirit again. Then draw the circle around the pentagram in a clockwise or sunwise direction (Wiccans call this deosil).

To banish something draw the pentagram in the opposite direction. Draw a line from earth, to water, to air, to fire, to spirit and then back to earth. then finish by drawing the circle around it in an anti-clockwise motion (Wiccans call this widdershins).

The pentagram can also be used in magic when you wish to call upon an element. Draw the pentagram clockwise (deosil) from the opposite side of the element point, finishing the pentagram at the point of the element you wish to invoke. To banish an element, start at the point of the element, continue anti-clockwise (widdershins) and finish off the pentagram at the opposite point.

This is useful to draw upon the elemental powers, or to remove the powers. Each element has a colour; water is blue, fire is red, earth is green, air is yellow and spirit is white, so when invoking or banishing an element it is best to draw it with the colour element you are invoking or banishing, or, if you are drawing your pentagram in the air with a wand, athame or your finger, then visualise the element colour when drawing the pentagram. There are many reasons you may wish to invoke or banish a certain element. You may want to banish the emotional attachment of the water element; this would be called severing a bond. You may wish to invoke the strength of the fire element to you. Think of the attributes each element has and try to use them in your magic by invoking and banishing. Learn the pentagram points and the elements attributed to each point. It may seem complicated at first but it isn't hard to get the hang of and can be very useful.

The Inverted Pentagram

The pentagram with the point upwards is a symbol of the Goddess and divine feminine, while the inverted pentagram, with the point directed downwards, is a sign of the God and male energies. When the pentagram is pointing upwards it is pointing to the heavens and the Goddess, but when it is pointing downwards it is pointing to earth and the male energies. The inverted pentagram has been given a bad name through the years as it has been seen as a symbol of devil worship or other negative symbols. Although this may be the case for some people it is not the case in Wicca as we have no devil. Remember, the devil is a Christian concept. When the pentagram is inverted it has a goat-like face with horns. In Wicca we have horned male Gods known as Pan and Cernunnos, Gods of everything wild and of the forest, consorts of the Goddess. But because these Gods have horns and hoofed feet they have been likened to the Christian devil. Be assured, this is not true; Pan and Cernunnos are not demon like or evil in the slightest, they are the keepers of the earth, loving and generous. In Gardnerian and Alexandrian Wicca the inverted pentagram is symbol for the initiation of a second degree witch. It represents the darker earthly masculine side that the second degree witch must learn to control in order to stop it rising up and exerting too much power as they themselves become more powerful.

"We have finally started to notice that there is real curative value in local herbs and remedies. In fact, we are also becoming aware that there are little or no side effects to most natural remedies, and that they are often more effective than Western medicine"

Anne Wilson-Schaef

Herbs

Herbs have been used for thousands of years in magic and healing and consequently some are sacred to certain Gods and Goddesses. Like people, they have different essences; in extreme cases they can drive a cat crazy (catnip), they can make you feel relaxed and joyful (cannabis) and can even poison you if you're not careful. Some herbs offer their user feelings of euphoria and are therefore extremely addictive, such as the cocoa plant, which is the basis for cocaine, whilst other herbs simply need to grow in your garden to bring luck and fortune to you.

There are numerous ways you can use herbs in your magical workings:

Bath

You can sprinkle herbs straight into your bath, such as rose petals or leaves of a plant, or you can make a sachet of herbs and let it soak in your bath like a tea bag, such as eucalyptus, for help with your sinuses. Lavender meanwhile will draw love to you or protect you.

Oils

You can use essential oils in magic for all types of things. You can make potions with them, put them on your skin to get rid of scars or burns, anoint a candle with them, burn them for aromatherapy or add them to your bath. You can also make your own oils by adding herbs to olive, almond or coconut oil. These can be used for anointing candles, for a bath, for beauty, hair or nails treatment or simply flavoursome and health-giving oils for cooking.

Tincture

Tinctures are a form of herbal medicine, often made with alcohol to preserve and extract the herb's goodness. You can also make tinctures with cider vinegar or honey. To make a basic tincture, fill a glass jar or bottle with herbs and then pour alcohol over the top until it reaches the top. The best alcohol to use is often said to be vodka, because it's colourless, odourless and fairly flavourless. Other spirits can be used however. The most important factor is that the alcohol is at least 80 proof (40% alcohol) to prevent mildewing of the plant material in the bottle. Put the lid on tightly and leave for at least three weeks, making sure to turn it or shake it at least once a day. Finally, strain the liquid into a dark coloured bottle, preferably blue, and you have your medicine. It is usually recommended to take two tablespoons of tincture in the day and two at night but it really depends on the herb and what it is for. If your purpose is to aid sleep you would only take a spoonful at night, but if it's a tonic, you would only take it in the morning.

Poultice

A poultice, also called cataplasm, is made by mashing the herb, either with a heavy object or pestle and mortar to make a paste, sometimes heated, that is spread on cloth over skin to treat an aching, inflamed, or painful part of the body, or to draw out pus from infected wounds, and remove embedded particles and foreign articles from the skin such as splinters.

Burning

Many herbs can be dried out and burned as incense. Sage, rosemary and sweetgrass make excellent smudge sticks for burning and getting rid of negative energy or unwanted entities. Of course, you can also buy incense sticks instead of making them.

Teas

Herbal teas have many health benefits; you can infuse some choice herbs in boiling water to make any number of teas. The correct word for herbal tea is tisane. You can make a variety of tisane's, such a chamomile for aiding sleep, or lemon and honey for a sore throat.

Spreading

Certain herbs can be spread around your altar, home or garden to ward off incoming bad luck or to attract love, luck or money.

Sachets

Place herbs in a little sachet to take with you for luck or protection. Other herbs can give you confidence or even attract money. Sachets are usually made from material or muslin cloth, tied with a ribbon at the top. You can also put one on your bed to aid sleep.

Below is a list of the most commonly used herbs in magic and healing. Be aware that the healing effects of herbs are in no way a substitute for going to see a medical doctor; always consult a doctor before using herbs for medical complaints. The information given is solely for information purposes and not intended to give medical advice. Use what follows as the base for further research.

Angelica Root

This herb is used in an incense smudge stick to clear a space of negative or stale energies. You can also carry it with you inside a sachet for protection. Add it to your bath to remove negative energies and give you a sense of calm. Use it to aid digestion if you feel blocked up or to elevate a build-up of phlegm due to cold. Do not use if pregnant.

Basil

Basil is used in love spells; sprinkle it into your bath to attract love and put leaves under your lover's pillow to help with fertility. It can be burned as a smudge stick to disperse negative energies, can stop vomiting through chewing and is a relaxant when used as a tea. Make an oil to prevent ageing and rub on wounds to stop infection as it has great anti-bacterial and fungicidal properties. Basil can also be used to stop stomach upsets such as constipation and is also very good for clearing the lungs if you have asthma or bronchitis.

Bay Leaves

Bay leaves are excellent for bringing you luck. Write a wish on a bay leaf, then burn it over a white candle for your wish to come true (but remember not to wish for anything silly or too big, as the more achievable the wish the more chance it will have of coming true). Put bay leaves underneath your pillow at night to induce prophetic dreaming. Drop them around your home and leave for a few hours before sweeping them out to cleanse your house of negativity. Add to teas to relieve stomach cramps.

Blessed Thistle

Carry this around with you in a sachet or blend with other protective herbs as a protector. Put in teas to help relieve migraine and headaches. A good blood purifier, many use it as a diuretic, for increasing urine output, and for promoting the flow of breast milk in new mothers. Don't confuse with milk thistle.

Burdock

This can be burned to cleanse a space away from anyone wanting to cause you harm. Infuse in tea for alleviating arthritis pain, removing toxins from the body and for skin problems. Burdock is also used for sore throats and colds and it's even reported to be successful in dealing with chronic diseases such as cancers, diabetes and AIDS.

Bramble (Blackberry) Leaf

Use this to invoke the Celtic Goddess Brigid. Grow it to attract faeries to your garden. Combined with Ivy and Rowan it makes a powerful spell to get rid of evil or anyone wanting to cause you harm. Put the three of them into a sachet and carry it with you or hang the sachet in your home.

Cacao Beans

Chocolate in its pure form was used extensively by the Aztecs who called it Food of the Gods. It is extremely effective in love potions, is a euphoric and can treat depression. Bitterer than processed chocolate, the beans are amazingly healthy and many people incorporate them into their daily diet, as they are said to be able to fight off cancers and are packed with vitamin C. Use them as an offering to the Gods and they will look upon you favourably.

Camellia

The leaves of the Camellia plant are used for green tea, oolong tea and black tea, all of which have well known health properties, including vitamins, minerals and antioxidants. However, you can buy the leaves before they have gone through this preparation or buy them in capsule form. Put the leaves into water on your altar on a full moon to attract good luck and money

107

to yourself. Crush them into a paste and add a little coconut oil to deal with skin conditions such as eczema.

Caraway

Also known as meridian fennel or Persian cumin, caraway has aphrodisiac properties when taken as a tea. An integral part of the Indian cuisine, Carry it in a sachet with you for luck and protection or use in spells to ensure faithfulness.

Carob

You can burn this herb to detract poltergeists as they hate carob smoke. Carry it with you for protection. Use as a healthier, caffeine free alternative to hot chocolate as the tastes are extremely similar.

Catnip

Having trouble sleeping? Use this herb in a tea to make you feel sleepy or relaxed. Cats love catnip as it has the same effect on them too, and it's also effective with infections and fevers as it aids perspiration. Burn as incense to draw love towards you.

Cayenne Pepper

This herb gives extra power to any spell, so is always worth considering. Use it for getting rid of bad energies and sprinkle it over your doorway to dissuade selected people from entering your home. Take a teaspoon full in hot water to remove plaque built up on arteries. Especially good for those who have suffered a heart attack or are in danger of doing so, as it can lower blood pressure and cholesterol when incorporated into your diet. Research shows that capsaicin, an active ingredient inside cayenne and other peppers, causes cancer cells to kill themselves in a process known as apoptosis. It is good for arthritis pain, and can be made into a paste and put on aching joints topically.

Cedar

Use cedar in spells when you want things brought to you, such as money, luck and love. Burn cedar in your bedroom to stop unwanted night terrors and keep it in your wallet or purse to attract money. A strong disinfectant, it's also particularly effective for treating colds and bronchial conditions. Infusing leaves into a tea helps with skin conditions such as athlete's foot and ringworm.

Chamomile

Drink chamomile in herbal tea as a relaxant for muscles and nerves and to aid sleep; it will help you fall asleep and continue working throughout the night. Effective for stomach aches and cramps, for pre-menstrual tension and excessive gas, you can also put chamomile in your bath to attract love.

Cinnamon

Cinnamon is a male aphrodisiac, both the scent and when put into foodstuff. It can be burnt to attract luck, money and love or ground into a powder and made into a sachet for luck. Take it with you to job interviews or on a new business venture. When added to honey, cinnamon makes a powerful medicine, relieving arthritis and bladder infections and lowering cholesterol. If you have heart problems make a paste using equal parts honey and cinnamon and add to brown toast and eat daily. Use the same combination to combat stomach ulcers, stomach upsets and even stomach cancer, as well as bone cancer. For bad breath gargle a mixture of honey and cinnamon as it prevents bacteria growing in your mouth.

Cloves

Use as incense to attract money and good luck. To stop people gossiping about you, burn as incense and say, "gossip be gone, close your mouth, I send this smoke to you from this house, no more hurt or lies for me, this is my will so mote it be," and let the incense drift out the window. Hang gloves over a baby's cot (not directly above it in case one falls off and is ingested by the baby) for protection. Cloves are extremely high in antitoxins; drink in teas for a detox of poisons from the body and to stop diarrhoea and vomiting. They are also a natural antiseptic, so use clove oil on cuts and grazes, on athletes' foot, burns and wounds.

Coltsfoot

Add this to a sachet and carry it around with you to find love. Coltsfoot was smoked in shamanic times to see visions and is excellent for any lung problems (its nickname is coughwort), including coughs, bronchitis and whooping cough. For any chest disorder add one tablespoon to a pint of boiling water, allow to steep for thirty minutes and then take a cloth or cotton wool and rub it on the chest and throat to expel mucus. Do not drink the potion; this is only for external use. And do not use when pregnant or nursing.

Cumin

Salt is excellent for expelling bad energies and evil, and mixing it with cumin gives it an extra punch. Make a circle of protection around yourself when meditating. When you move to a new house or if your house has bad energies, put a cumin and salt mix in every corner of every room and leave for one day, then sweep it up and bury it in the earth. Put cumin seeds in wine as an aphrodisiac. It can also help with flatulence, indigestion, atonic dyspepsia, nausea, morning sickness, diarrhoea and the common cold. In these cases, the seeds are boiled in water to make a tea, using one teaspoon of seeds per cup of water.

Comfrey Leaves

This herb is used in travelling spells; give to a person travelling long distances for a safe journey, or if you are nervous about meeting someone take a comfrey leaf with you. For treating spots and acne, cold sores, irritated skin, bug bites or stings, steep one part comfrey leaves with two parts boiling water and let steep for twenty minutes, before applying with cotton wool. Alternatively, make into a tea and then pour into a bath to help with sore bones or muscles.

Damiana

Damiana is a herb for love, lust and passion, a wonderful aphrodisiac. Make a tea with the herb for lust and in sex magic. It is also the best herb for hangovers and when smoked has a marijuana like effect, but much milder.

Dandelion Leaves

Use dandelion root in tea for relaxation and to aid sleep. You can also use the whole thing - root, leaves and flower - and put it in a sachet next to your pillow. A great herb for chasing away nightmares and encouraging sweet dreams.

Dill

Dill has been used for thousands of years as a protection herb. Grow it in your garden to bring peace to your home. Take a sachet and hang it in your hallway or carry a sachet for luck and protection. Use as a tea and add to your bath, and while lying in the bath think of the person you desire to attract them towards you. Dill is an appetizer; just smelling it makes you hungry, especially if you have been off your food or want to make someone eat. Make dill tea to aid sleep as it has a hypnotic effect on the body. Chew dill to expel trapped gas or cure hiccups.

Eucalyptus Leaf

Use this herb in harmony spells; mash into a paste, put it on every finger, stick your fingers together and say, "heal this rift I have with (persons full name), mend the bridges burned and bring peace back to both of our lives." Now meditate on this for a few minutes and wash off the paste. Eucalyptus is also an excellent germ killer, with natural antiseptic qualities. Use a few drops of oil in a bath or in water to clear sinuses, whilst bought in supplement form from a chemist or health food shop it can be excellent for boosting your immune system.

Fennel Seeds

Use in spell work to protect you from curses or hexes or from anyone wanting to cause you harm. Drink fennel tea for gas and stomach upsets. Fennel tea is also excellent for people with lung problems such as a cough or bronchitis. Mothers who drink fennel tea find their babies have a much less chance from suffering from colic than mothers who don't drink it, and it also promotes milk production for nursing mothers.

Feverfew

Feverfew is the herb of the traveller and you should always keep a sachet of this herb in your car for protection. Take it with you on holiday or on long journeys. Grow feverfew to ward off sickness. Make as a tea to ward off migraine; it opens blood flow to the head and can stop migraines from coming on, and it also reduces sensitivity to light and nausea.

Flax Seeds

Flax seeds are used to drain away negativity. Add them to a bowl and leave them in the centre of your home to absorb bad or negative energies. Carry flax seeds in your wallet or purse to attract money. Flax seeds are extremely high in Omega 3 fatty acids, beneficial to keeping a healthy heart and lowering cholesterol.

Garlic

Garlic is the herb of Goddess Hecate. Use it to ward off evil and keep a string of garlic in your kitchen to attract happiness. Garlic has many healing properties and is what we call a super herb; it helps your body in many ways, from keeping a healthy heart and blood pressure, to boosting the immune system and lowering cholesterol. Use garlic in your diet as much as you can or take supplements to stay healthy.

Ginger

Eat ginger before performing spells to increase the power of the spell. Use in spells to do with luck, money and love. Ginger is used in healing because of its anti-inflammatory properties.

Inflammation is an underlying cause for many health issues so ensure ginger becomes an essential part of your diet. Make a healing ginger tea by boiling two dice sized cubes for about fifteen minutes with the lid on so as not to lose any of its healing properties.

Ginseng Powder

Use ginseng powder as an aphrodisiac tea, and use the root in spell work to attract new love. An excellent mood enhancer and anti-depressant, it helps with blood pressure and aids digestion.

Hibiscus Flower

Made into tea, hibiscus flower is a sexual potent potion. It is also enhances psychic powers and is good to have in a bath before any divination work. Use this plant in love spells and for weight loss as it gets rid of fluid retention. Particularly strong hibiscus tea can be a gentle laxative or pulp into paste for itchy or irritated skin and apply for a few minutes.

Holly

Holly is used to ward off any evil or negative forces; keep it near you or your home. The wood is often used for magical tools. Do not consume as it is poisonous if eaten.

Hops

Hops are fantastic as a sleep aid. Put them into a sachet and hang on your bed post, or take as a tea for a good night's sleep. Burn hops for healing spells or to meditate.

Horehound

This is an excellent pick me up herb; drink it as a tea to give you energy and to feel awake. This herb was called the Seed of Horus by the ancient Egyptians as it has strong protection qualities; carry it with you in a sachet for protection and luck. Gather wild horehound and tie it together with a red ribbon, then place it around your home for luck, prosperity and protection.

Hyssop

Hyssop is associated with serpents and dragons, so use this herb in spell work for invoking the power of dragons or for protection. Use in a tea for respiratory or congestion problems as it works wonderful if you have a cold and can also be drank to stop anxiety attacks. As a tincture take three teaspoons a day for colds, flu, bronchitis, anxiety, coughing, headaches, high blood pressure, digestive problems such as diarrhoea and indigestion, nausea and vomiting. But do not take when pregnant.

Juniper Berries

Good for banishing bad energies - carry it with you for luck and protection. Burn dried berries for a purifying incense and to increase psychic energies. Juniper berries are also used for urinary problems; they stimulate the urinary passages, making the kidneys move fluid faster. Take sparsely and in small doses. You can also apply juniper berries direct to the skin for aching muscles and joints.

Lemon and Lime

Use lime or lemons as a natural deodorant; just cut a slice and rub it into your underarms and it works better than most bought deodorants and is far healthier. Make a tea of lemon and hot water to flush out toxins and drink every morning. Lemon and honey in a tea or tincture will combat a sore throat. Use lemon or lime and water as a natural hairspray, one part lemon juice to two parts water. Use the juice of two lemons together with one cup of water to lighten your hair.

Mandrake Root

Mandrake is very magical; to fully charge it sleep with it under your bed for three nights, then use in any magical spells to intensify the magic. Carry it with you for courage. According to ancient legend, when the root is dug up it screams and kills all who hear it. However, a whole mandrake root in your home will bring protection and prosperity. When used as a tea mandrake is a hallucinogen, but do not ingest as it is a narcotic and can be very dangerous indeed.

Morning Glory Blossoms

Use in a sachet and put under your pillow to induce blissful dreams. This herb was sacred to the Aztecs. Do not ingest as this plant is toxic if eaten.

Moss

Put moss on the earth quarter of your altar to enhance your spell work.

Mugwort

It has been said that mugwort, associated with the Greek Moon Goddess Artemis, can bring you dreams of the future. Put a sachet of it under your pillow for prophetic dreams. Burn with sandlewood or wormwood to bring on visions, or alternatively make as a tea with a little honey.

Mullein

Mullein is known as the witches' torch and is said to illuminate any spells you perform. Keep some with you for protection and burn it to expel demons or a bad presence. Use in a tea or tincture for cold and flu symptoms, bronchitis and coughs, ear infections and stomach cramps. Apply the oil directly to skin rashes or burns for instant relief. It will also have sedative effect when drank as a tea 10 minutes before bed.

Nettles

Sprinkle nettles around your home to expel any negativity or unwanted presence. Use in a bath to wash away negativity that has become stuck to you throughout the day. Nettles have many healing properties and are one of the nine Anglo-Saxon sacred herbs. Make into a strong tea or tincture to relieve arthritis and destroy intestinal worms. Drink nettle tea when pregnant to ensure a healthy baby as it is rich in minerals and vitamin K and controls bleeding. It also promotes milk for nursing mothers, is rich in iron and can help with fatigue and anaemia. Use nettle to get rid of bad skin problems such as acne and eczema and use the tea upon your head to stimulate hair growth and restore natural hair colour.

Nutmeg

Use in spells for money and wealth. Nutmeg is a hallucinogen when made into a tea, having a psychedelic effect, but it can be toxic in large doses, so only a small sprinkle would be needed. If you've not used it before grind half a nut into 750 ml of water and simmer over a stove for an hour without letting it boil. Drink while warm and mixed with honey as it tastes quite awful.

Orris Root

Orris Roots and leaves hung in your home are excellent for protection and keeping people out who wish to do you harm. Turn the root into a powder and on a waxing moon, offer the powder to Aphrodite as an offering to bring love into your life. Orris root as a scent or oil is perfect for attracting a lover.

Pau D'Arco

This herb is used in a 'drawing down the moon' ritual as an offering. Ask that the moon be drawn down into the herb for healing. Make a tea using the inner bark (the outer bark has almost no medicinal purpose) by adding one ounce to a pint of boiling water and leaving to steep for twenty minutes. If made into a tincture, take two teaspoons two times a day. This will treat many illnesses. Pau D'Arco is antibiotic, antifungal, antitumor, antiviral, diuretic, digestive, anodyne, ant-stringent, parasiticide and hypertensive. It is also a potent tonic and cell rejuvenator.

Passion Flower

Use passion flower in spell work to attract partnerships or friendships and promote emotional balance. Infuse as tea for calming if you are nervous or to aid in sleep. Additionally, many people who suffer seizures claim passion flower is very beneficial.

Pennyroyal

Carry with you in a green bag to attract luck and money. Take with you on business ventures or job interviews. Burn for protection. However, do not ever consume, and especially when pregnant, as it can stimulate menstruation and cause miscarriage.

Peppermint

Place peppermint in a sachet under your pillow to promote sweet dreams. Use in spell work for purification and healing. Burn as an incense to promote happiness and before a big event to ensure its success. Use peppermint capsules to relieve digestive problems. Drink as a tea for cold and flu, irritable bowel syndrome, indigestion and heartburn.

Pine

Pine is an evergreen so use it in spells for strength. Burn the wood and needles for protective incense or to alleviate feelings of guilt. The pine needles made into a tea are very rich in vitamin C and can loosen the feelings of a tight chest as the tea and scent open up your lungs and breathing passages.

Raspberry Leaves

Raspberry leaves are to be used in spells of love and to promote visions in dreams. Made as a tincture or tea they can stop vomiting and diarrhoea and are also good for kidney health.

Rose Petals

Use rose petals for spells involving love, romance and protection and for keeping harmony within the home. If roses are grown in your garden they will bring peace towards you. Use petals in a tincture, oil or tea to relieve headaches and menstrual cramps. They are also a good heart and nerve tonic.

Rosehip

Tie rosehips together like beads and wear as a necklace to attract love and protection. Rosehips are high in Vitamins A, B, C and K and also contain iron and pectin so are highly beneficial when drunk as a tea or tincture. Use for overall health and wellbeing.

Rosemary

Burn rosemary as a smudge stick to purify and cleanse yourself, your home or someone else's home. Use in spells for love, protection, lust and prosperity. Make rosemary oil by adding sprigs to either olive, almond or coconut oil and infusing for two weeks. You can then use this to anoint candles for spell work. Rosemary also has many health benefits when made into a tea or tincture or simply added to your diet. It can heal depression, give you a little buzz of energy, relieve headaches and halitosis and help with your memory. Chew rosemary for relief from coughs or chest infections. Make a rosemary dolly to bring you luck; just fashion sprigs of rosemary into arms, legs and a head and bind together with white ribbon.

Sage

Use sage as a smudge stick to purify your home and get rid of stale or negative energies, or to chase away bad spirits. It can be used with rosemary, sweetgrass or both to make the smudging stronger. To the Native Americans sage was one of the gifts from the Great Spirit and was a powerful purifier in many of their rituals. The Romans cleansed themselves and dressed in white before ritualistically harvesting sage with special silver tools. The Greeks used sage as a brain tonic. In English the word 'sage' means someone who is wise. Use in spell work for healing and money spells and carry in sachets for protection and luck. Use sage as a tea with lemon to cure coughs or colds and lower blood sugars. Make a lotion for problematic skin with one and half cups of fresh sage leaves, one litre of water, ten cloves and two star anise. Simmer in a pan for fifteen minutes, stirring often, let it cool and then strain the liquid using a sieve. Now add the lotion to a spray bottle or one with a cork. Use as a refreshing spray or with cotton wool for acne, oily or uneven skin.

Salt

Although not a herb, salt is much used in all aspects of magical workings and has been used by many religions throughout history. Use rock salt as a representation of earth on your altar's north quarter, or use sea salt as a representation of water in the west quarter. Salt is a protector as it absorbs negative energies; put it in every corner of your home and leave it there for twenty four hours, then sweep it up and bury it. If you make a circle of salt and go inside the circle no bad or negative energies can hurt you. You can do this when meditating. You can also make holy water with salt by doing the following: put water into a bowl and place your hands over the water and say, "I exorcise this water from impurities, bless this water oh Goddess divine." Then take the salt and put your hand over it and say, "I exorcise this salt from any impurities in the name of the divine God." Now pour salt into the water (approx. one part salt for three parts water) and stir the salt around the bowl clockwise until the salt is dissolved. Finally, put your hand over the water and say, "I consecrate this water to work through the divine and cleanse all it touches, so be it." To give the water extra strength undertake this ritual on a full moon and make enough to last you until the next full moon.

Shavegrass

This herb is also known as horsetail and is very powerful in the use of fertility spells, so if you wish to conceive, keep it with you at all times. Shavegrass is one of the richest plant sources of silica known to man - silica coverts to calcium in the human body. Use it to strengthen bones and prevent skin from wrinkling, and for any urinary infections or kidney stones, make into a tea or tincture.

Seaweed

Seaweed can be used on your altar to represent water in your west quarter. Use it in magic to summon sea spirits. If you start a new business rub seaweed on the doors and windows to attract customers. Keep it in a sachet and carry it around with you to attract money. Seaweed has many health benefits and can be introduced to your diet and eaten often to keep you fit and healthy. Don't just head down to your local beach though as not every type of seaweed is edible.

St John's Wart

Also known as tipton's weed, rosin rose, goatweed, chase-devil or klamath weed, you can use this in magic to rid yourself of negative energy. Drink as a tea to fight depression. This herb was sacred to the druids; they would make it into a necklace and wear it to ward off sickness.

Star Anise

Star Anise is an excellent herb to dispel negativity and evil; if you're suffering from bad dreams keep a sachet under your pillow. Before meditation inhale its scent deep within you to increase visions and psychic powers. For thousands of years the Japanese planted star anise around sacred temples and in grace yards to consecrate and bring protection. Buddhists plant them around their temples for the same reason. Burn the seeds to bring on psychic visions and for protection. Make a necklace to wear or hang around your home. Drink as a tea or make a tincture for coughs cold and flu or as a remedy for flatulence and nausea. Chew the seeds after meals to aid digestion.

Thyme

Burn thyme as incense for healing spell work, wear it and put it in your bath to increase your psychic energy. The name thyme comes from the Greek word thymus, meaning courage. Keep in a sachet with you if you are doing something you may need extra strength for. Ancient Egyptians used it in the mummification process. Make a poultice by mashing the leaves up and treat skin infections with them; it's also good for athletes' foot. Because it has many powers, thyme can be used as an antiseptic, anodyne, disinfectant, antitussive, anti-inflammatory, rubefacient, demulcent, carminative, diaphoretic, depurative, digestive, diuretic, expectorant, fungicide, nervine, pectoral, sedative, stimulant, and vermifuge. For all these benefits simply make it into a tea or tincture or add it to your diet.

Valerian Root

Valerian is a brilliant balancer; grow it in your home or garden to keep an important balance around you. Use in dream magic and drink in tea or take as supplements for aiding sleep. It can also help with depression. Drink a cup of tea nightly before bed, but use in moderation.

Vanilla

Use vanilla in love spells, and for seduction. Take a sachet with you to attract love. Wear oil as a fragrance and as an aphrodisiac. On a full moon, ask the Love Gods to send love towards you and then wear something with a vanilla scent for the following two weeks to bring love your way.

White Willow Bark

Use in spells for protection, love and money. Carry in a sachet to attract love and dispel negativity and burn with sandalwood to conjure good spirits. Use to bring blessings of the moon to you. Aspirin's main ingredient can be found in white willow bark; chew it for relief from headaches, period pains, toothaches, muscle and joints soreness, as well as colds and flu. It can also be made into a tea or a tincture.

Yarrow Root

Named after the Greek God Achilles, yarrow root is excellent for ridding negative energies and depression. Use in magic to dispel evil or bad feelings and carry as an amulet to keep away anyone wanting to do you harm. Also known as woundwort, it has long been used to stop bleeding when applied to a wound and was carried in battle and wars right up to the Second World War. Use as a tea to induce sweating to relieve fevers. Sooth toothache and sore gums by either chewing or making a tincture and rubbing into gums. Yarrow is also good for stimulating cell re-growth and is said to be a brilliant tonic for hair loss, so make into a tincture and rub on the head before normal shampooing. It should be avoided if pregnant and can have a reaction when using other drugs such as blood thinners or blood pressure drugs. Consult your doctor if you use medical drugs. Some people may be allergic so, as with the use of any herb, and especially in the early stages, use with caution.

"Every particular in nature, a leaf, a drop, a crystal, a moment of time is related to the whole, and partakes of the perfection of the whole"

Ralph Waldo Emerson

Gems, Stones and Crystals

Coming straight from the heart of the earth and encompassing all the elements, gems, stones and crystals have massive amounts of magical and healing properties, as well as enormous amounts of energy, all filled with different vibrations. Indeed, everything in the universe runs at different vibrations and frequencies; if you looked at the world through a powerful microscope you would see everything held together by tiny little particles pulling together to form shapes. Because of the toughness and hardness in gems, stones and crystals we believe these energies or vibrations are stronger than almost anything else because of the energy created by the molecules holding them together, such as magnetism. It is the energy they vibrate at that enhances healing, both physical and emotional.

For thousands of years numerous cultures and tribes have believed in these magical and healing properties. Jewellery wasn't worn simply because it looked pretty; it was also worn as a talisman for many different reasons, from bringing luck to warding off evil spirits.

Birth Stones

Certain stones are attributed to the date you were born. These are called birth stones, and it is said you should always carry a piece of your birth stone to bring you luck. Birth stones are attributed to the Gregorian calendar and there have been many ancient songs and poems around these stones. This is a poem first printed by Tiffany & Co. in 1870 by an unknown author. It's said to be an ancient poem passed down through ages.

By her who in this month (January) is born
No gem save Garnets should be worn
They will ensure her constancy
True friendship, and fidelity

The February-born shall find
Sincerity and peace of mind
Freedom from passion and from care
If they an *Amethyst* will wear

Who in this world of ours their eyes
In March first open shall be wise
In days of peril firm and brave
And wear a *Bloodstone* to their grave

She who from April dates her years
Diamonds shall wear, lest bitter tears
For vain repentance flow; this stone
Emblem of innocence, is known

Who first beholds the light of day
In spring's sweet flowery month of May
And wears an *Emerald* all her life
Shall be a loved and happy wife

Who comes with summer to this earth
And owes to June her hour of birth
With ring of *Agate* on her hand
Can health, wealth, and long life command

The glowing *Ruby* shall adorn
Those who in July are born
Then they'll be exempt and free
From love's doubts and anxiety

Wear a *Sardonyx* or for thee
No conjugal felicity
The *August*-born without this stone
'Tis said, must live unloved and lone

A maiden born when September leaves
Are rustling in September's breeze
A *Sapphire* on her brow should bind
'Twill cure diseases of the mind.

October's child is born for woe
And life's vicissitudes must know
But lay an *Opal* on her breast
And hope will lull those woes to rest

Who first comes to this world below
With drear November's fog and snow

119

Should prize the Topaz's amber hue
Emblem of friends and lovers true

If cold December gave you birth
The month of snow and ice and mirth
Place on your hand a Turquoise blue
Success will bless whatever you do

Below is a list of stones, gems and crystals with their healing and magical meanings. Remember that colours are very important and notice many come in a variety of different colours whilst others are multi coloured. See the chapter on colours for further information. Before using gems, stones and crystals in spells or rituals, wash them to remove any unwanted vibrations and to prepare them to receive your intentions. Cleanse them in running water with mild soap and visualize white light permeating the stones and clearing them.

And please note: there are thousands of different gems, stones and crystals - this is a list of some of the most commonly used. Research further for even more information about any you are particularly interested in.

Agate

Agate is a very hard but beautiful stone, coming in almost all colours of the rainbow, and arranged into fascinating circles and stripes. Mainly found in India, Brazil, Uruguay and North America, it's a good all round protector that's connected to the mind and can be worn for help relating to mental health issues and depression. Popular in Feng Shui, agate is also related to new beginnings and so this stone is beneficial for new homes or new ventures.

Amazonite

Named after the Amazon River and said to have adorned the shields of the famous Amazonian female warriors, amazonite is beautiful, blue and useful for balance and harmonising yourself. If you feel things are too chaotic in your life use amazonite to bring back some stability. Sleep with it under your pillow so that it can help you understand the symbolism of your dreams and place it near microwaves, computers and cell phones to block geopathic stress and electromagnetic pollution.

Amber

Fossilised tree resin famed and used since Neolithic times, amber was written about by Pliny the Elder. He recounted Nicias' view of it being "a liquid produced by the rays of the sun; and that these rays, at the moment of the sun's setting, striking with the greatest force upon the surface of the soil, leave upon it an unctuous sweat, which is carried off by the tides of the ocean, and thrown up upon the shores of Germany." Most amber these days comes from Russia and the Baltic, from trees that fossilized 37 to 42 million years ago. It is a provider of strength, to be used when you need some energy or you need to feel stronger or more confident about something. It also helps with the eyes, nose and throat in healing.

Amethyst

Amethyst is a violet coloured variety of quartz, named after the Ancient Greek's belief it protected its owner from drunkenness. Found mainly in North and South America and Russia, it is a psychic 'semi-precious' stone that opens the mind to pathways of the supernatural and helps healers to focus. It is also a cleansing stone and can be used to cleanse a space for your tools. Put amethysts on your windowsill to receive the sun and help with healing and to receive the moonlight at night time to bring calmness.

Apache Tear

Volcanic black glass opaque by reflected light but translucent when held up to the light, the name comes from Apache warriors who rode their horses over a mountainside rather than be killed by the US cavalry. When their wives and children cried their tears turned to stone upon hitting the ground. Found in Mexico and South Western USA, apache tears are stones for grounding, protection and ridding yourself of negative emotions. They are particularly useful for healers because they strengthen the blood and the immune system and aid in the removal of toxins.

Aquamarine

Found in Sri Lanka, Madagascar, North and South America and Africa, the name Aquamarine is Latin for 'water of the sea.' It was said to be the treasure of mermaids and was a talisman for courage. Sailors used to carry them at sea to prevent drowning. It is a stone of emotional balance and clarity, so use it when things feel they are getting out of control and it will help bring back harmony in your life. Place it in water which is bathed in sunlight. Use it for courage and peace and in healing, for your nerves and for fluid retention, kidneys and thyroid.

Bloodstone / Heliotrope

Usually dark green with red spots of blood, this stone is mainly found in India, Brazil, China, Australia and the United States. Bloodstone is used to bring things towards you. It can attract money, luck and love, and is best used on a waxing moon. As its name suggests, bloodstone is good to help with blood issues, such as nosebleeds, bad circulation, menstrual cycles etc.

Blue Chalcedony

A member of the quartz family, use this crystal to engage courage, uplift the spirit and bring yourself or others back down to reality. Known as the Speaker's Stone, the Roman orator Cicero wore one around his neck. Considered sacred by Native American Indians, chalcedony eases self-doubt and brings inner calm through periods of reflection.

Calcite

A common mineral in many different forms and colours, calcite is used to increase the power of any project you are doing. Use in meditation to clear the mind and rid yourself of self-doubt, or to clear a room of negativity.

Carnelian

The colour of a deep sunset or the first flushes of autumn, use carnelian as a protector and as a talisman to ward off negativity, hexes or curses. Alchemists used it as a boiling stone to increase the power of all other ingredients. It is good for passion and blood issues, especially sexually, such as impotency. Users should put the stone on their groin for an hour each day to increase blood flow to the penis.

Citrine

Most citrine bought today is actually modified amethyst. Real citrine is not a burnt orange yellow colour but instead a gentle yellow. Use it to instil confidence in oneself. Citrine is a masculine stone and is said to hold energy of the sun within it, so it is a good all round healer and protector. Excellent to wear as a talisman for protection and good health.

Chrysocolla

Chrysocolla, a stone of emotions that can ease a broken heart, has colours of amazing depth and is used to attract love. Mainly found in Chile, Russia and Zaire, keep it next to your bed at night to bring sweet dreams. It promotes clarity of thought and, in healing, cools fevers, detoxifies the liver and lowers blood pressure.

Diamond

Diamonds are probably the most well-known of the gem stones for their toughness and clarity. The name comes from the Ancient Greek word 'adamas', meaning unbreakable. Mined in India for six thousand years, diamonds relatively near earth's surface and therefore mineable are between one and three billion years old. However, not all diamonds found on earth originated here; some have arrived via asteroids and white dwarf stars. They are excellent as a meditation tool and good for cleansing an area and creating a positive space. Linked with the sexual organs and reproduction, they are also good to use in any of these issues.

Emerald

The emerald is the stone of Venus and brings love and positivity if you wear it. Used in spells of beauty and love, they also aid in reproduction. It's said if an emerald is given as a gift to a lover they will stay faithful to you. A beautiful green colour, sold in the markets of Babylon and worshiped by the Incas, they are also said to help eyesight and strengthen memory and brain function.

Garnet

A garnet is a feminine stone connected to the Moon Goddess and used to call her on a full moon. When meditating on beauty and guidance, hold a garnet for answers to your questions. Usually coloured deep red to purple, used in issues of menstrual cycles and reproduction and as an aid to your creativity, garnets obtained by deceit are said to bring a curse upon the thief until they are returned to the rightful owners.

Hematite

Streaked with rust-red and named after the Greek word for blood, hematite is a psychic stone, used to clear and balance the mind before doing any kind of divination or psychic workings. Used by early man for writing on cave walls, it is useful for solving problems and for protection, especially in the home, Hematite is also good aiding treatment of blood disorders, fevers and infections. Magnetic hematite is derived from natural hematite, titanium, copper and aluminium and is used by many people to relieve pain, restore energy, restore balance and enhance sleep.

Jade

Jade, a stone of healing and balance, brings a calming effect when held or placed upon the body. A stone of truth, keep jade on you at all times if you want to bring truth to the surface. It is also a stone of love and sensuality and since ancient times the Chinese have carved it into a butterfly to draw love towards the holder.

Jasper

Jasper means 'spotted or speckled stone' in Old French and was a favourite gem in the ancient world, with its name traced back in Arabic, Persian, Hebrew, Assyrian, Greek and Latin. A type of quartz formed in sedimentary rock it comes in many colours and with various patterning and is a powerful stone in all things divination and psychic. Use to stay grounded while meditating and wear as a talisman for protection. It brings luck and good fortune and can be used in all health issues, ranging from cancer to the common cold. Place it on the affected area for at least one hour per day. Each type of jasper also has its own unique energy depending on its colour and properties.

Lapis Lazuli

An intense coloured blue stone found in the Himalayas and the Andes, lapis lazuli is a finder of forbidden knowledge, a powerful stone that can help greatly with opening your psychic eye and seeing what you were unable to see before. Meditate with the stone holding it on your third eye (the middle of the forehead between your eyes). Found at Neolithic burials ten thousand years ago and used on the funeral mask of King Tutankhamun, this stone is related to a higher state of consciousness and connected with the divine. In health, use it to treat depression and other mental health issues such as giving up addiction.

Lepidolite

Found in the United States and in Brazil, this soft lilac coloured stone is excellent for giving up addictions and other obsessive thinking, as well as stabilising mood swings. Wear as a talisman to bring change for the better if you feel stuck in a rut and need a shift. It can be laid directly on painful parts of the body and helps with nerve pain, sciatica and joint problems.

Malachite

A vibrant green colour, found deep underground in fractures, spaces and stalagmites, malachite is a calmness stone that can aid in sleep disorders and get rid of bad dreams when kept beside your bed. Use it for wishes and, when worn as a talisman, for bringing desires to you. A protection stone, particularly for travel, take it with you on aeroplanes.

Moonstone

As the name suggests moonstone is connected to full and new moons and the Goddess. Use it to gain wisdom and to strengthen your intuition, for psychic workings, rune casting and tarot reading. Found in many parts of the world and believed to have been born from solidified rays of the moon, it is reputed to be a traveller's stone and can, like malachite, be carried to bring good fortune. In health, the moonstone is used in reproduction, sexual issues and menstrual issues.

Pearl

Tears of the Gods? Or dewdrops filled with moonlight that fell to the ocean? We know the truth these days; that a pearl is born from an act of protection, when a foreign object is lodged within an oyster or other mollusc. And yet still they are Goddess gems; how could they not be? They bring wisdom and femininity and are used to attract money, luck and love.

Obsidian

When volcanic lava, hurled from the womb of mother earth, comes into contact with large masses of water it cools so quickly it doesn't have time to crystallise. The result is a black shiny stone called obsidian. A talisman for bringing issues to the fore, obsidian is used with anything that requires your intuition or with any psychic workings. It draws toxins out of the body, especially the liver, and draws negative energy into itself, protecting yourself and your surroundings. Remember to cleanse it thoroughly before and after use.

Onyx

A precious stone found in many different colours and many different parts of the world, the onyx is perhaps most usually thought of as being black. It is a powerful protection stone that dispels any negativity. Use when meditating to stay grounded and centred and to keep a place peaceful and happy.

Opal

Spectacularly beautiful, with flashes of red, blue and yellow, opal is a stone that absorbs the energy around it, whether that be positive or negative. If you go to a happy place take opal with you and it will absorb the energy from that place, then take the stone away with you to keep that energy with you (just cleanse the stone when you want to remove the energy). It is used for emotional healing rather than bodily healing.

Peridot

Bright green peridot emits a warm and friendly energy and is used to attract wealth and good luck. A volcanic gem that contains the same composition as molten magma, it is associated with the liver and cleansing of the body from toxins and poisons.

Rose Quartz

Rose Quartz is connected to the heart and emotions and is particularly good for those who've suffered from a broken heart or some other traumatic experience in their lives. Wear it to attract love and give it to someone as a symbol of your love. In healing it is good to use with matters of the skin or heart.

Smoky Quartz

Smoky Quartz is a filter and a trap for negativity; keep it with you or in your home to dispel any negativity that may be coming towards you. Sometimes lined with 'angel hairs' these golden streams of energy provide even greater power for clarity and healing.

Clear Quartz

Clear quartz, known as Ice of Eternity, brings higher power to any other crystal, gem or stone because of its ability to hold your thought or energies from elsewhere, added to the fact it vibrates with such strong energy. If you use a crystal put it together with clear quartz to make the vibration and energy of the stone stronger. Used to make silicon chips inside computers, it is a great crystal for both beginners and the experienced.

Rhodochrosite

In its purest form a rose-red colour, this stone brings balance, calm and peace to a space, is perfect for relaxing and meditation, and for promoting peace and sleep when kept by your bed. Argentina's national gemstone, the Inca's believed it was the blood of their former leaders, turned to stone.

Ruby

The ruby is one of the most powerful and magnificent stones in the universe. It was said to own a ruby would always bring contentment and peace. Kublai Khan was said to have offered a whole city in exchange for a beautiful ruby. Used in all protection spells and worn for attracting love and friendship as well as protection, it stimulates the heart and can be used in the treatment of fevers and heat disorders.

Sodalite

Sometimes confused with lapis lazuli because of its colour, sodalite is an emotional healer and a stone of courage and transformation. If you are recovering from difficulty or trying to change or grow use this stone as a talisman. It's especially good for new learning, for starting courses or going to college or university and is considered lucky for artists of all types, and in particular creative writers.

Staurolite

Often shaped like a cross because of something called crystal twinning, staurolite is a stone of good luck and good fortune and is worn as a talisman for protection. In healing, it protects from cramps and helps with the central nervous system.

Sugilite

Sugilite is a stone of magical and psychic uses that deals with your higher consciousness. Keep this stone close when doing a spell or ritual as it understands magic and gives its own power to any magical work dealing with will and intent. It is also said to help cancer sufferers by reducing any related emotional turmoil or despair.

Sapphire

A stone of wisdom, sapphires are used when contacting the spirits and for any divination workings. In healing they're connected to the third eye, allowing people to see deeper into their true selves. They're also great for the respiratory system, for throat or breathing issues. Hold the sapphire over the problem area for at least thirty minutes a day.

Tigers Eye

A physical and spiritual protector associated with shamans and warriors for centuries, tigers eye is often worn as a talisman and enhances overall physical health and well-being. Primarily found in South Africa, it provides mental focus and stimulus, helping you keep to any plans.

Topaz

Topaz is a messenger gem; tell it your desires and it will echo your message out to the universe. Said to be a gateway into other worlds, its power increases and decreases with the power of the moon. Use for healing aching joints, enhancing blood flow and aiding weight loss.

Tourmaline

Tourmaline is used to enhance brain activity and helps you see things with clarity whilst expelling negative thoughts and worries. Excellent for divination and scrying, it is also a good stone for balancing and harmonising body and mind.

Turquoise

Named after the Old French word for 'Turkish', turquoise is an excellent stone for healing mind, body and spirit. Use it to relax yourself and bring about balance in your life. In healing, use with any stomach or intestinal disorders.

Unakite

Unakite is a type of jasper mainly found in Unakas Mountains in North Carolina and used for healing your spiritual self and for encouraging visions. If you're feeling down or drawn away from your spiritual self, hold unakite for bringing back a spiritual balance.

Zircon

One of the heaviest gemstones and appearing in a range of colours, zircon is an overall healer, adding power when used with other crystals or herbs in spell working. Use for beauty or enhancing your looks, making you more attractive to someone. It is also a sexual healer and can be used as an aphrodisiac.

"It does not matter how long you are spending on the earth, how much money you have gathered or how much attention you have received. It is the amount of positive vibration you have radiated in life that matters"

Amit Ray

Chants and Incantations

Chants or incantations (also called invocations) are spoken word spells. When we chant it is a kind of praying - to the universe, the elements, the Gods and Goddesses. It shows the intent of what we want to bring to us, or what we want to achieve. We put this message out into the universe to let it be known and to manifest our want. Sometimes all we want is to install a message into ourselves. Chants or incantations can be said over and over or just the once. They can be used to invoke a certain power, spirit or element or just to give us a power or strength. And on others occasions, we do not chant to ask for anything but only to give gratitude for all that we already have.

Words are so powerful they can create wars, help someone fall in love you with you, lead others to hate you or change lives. Words have power, so much power, so use them wisely; constructing words isn't called spelling for nothing.

Chants and incantations can be said on their own or during ritual or spell work to give them more power and to make your intent clear. You can make up your own chants and incantations; they work better when they come from your own heart and spirit. However, to get you started, here are some chants you can use as a guide. Feel free to use them as they are or amend them as you wish.

Assistance Chant

Divine mother
Mother divine
Show me the way
Give me a sign

Bonding Spell

(said between two people whilst a token is given to each other)

With this spell I have spoken
May the love in my life be awoken
I ask you to take the offer of this token
And never let our bonds be broken.
So mote it be

Cleansing Chant

Cleanse this space, remove the past
Help me find happiness at long last
Fill this space with joy and love
Send your blessing from above

Cleansing Spell

(best done in the shower or bath or simply splashing
water over face and hands)

I cleanse myself of negative feelings
I wash away my selfishness
I wash away my self-doubting
I wash away my negative thinking of others
I wash away jealousy
I bathe myself in happiness
I allow self-acceptance into myself
I feel gratitude for all that I have
I will practice acceptance of others and will not judge

Divination Element Incantation

Burn fire, burn bright, pure vision come to me
Water so lucid, let my mind be free
Earth so strong, grant me your presence
As I breathe in air, grant me your essence

Element Incantation

Earth, Air, Fire and Water
Give your presence to me
Earth, Air, Fire and Water
Open up your spirit to me
Earth, Air, Fire and Water
Lend your energy to me
Earth, Air, Fire and Water
Grant your power to me

Forgiveness Chant

(When we forgive someone we do not do it so the other person can feel better about what they have done; we forgive to let go of the past and bring ourselves peace. Try your best to forgive as clinging onto anger and fear will only hurt you further)

Anger and hurt, stress and strife
I won't allow these to control my life
I forgive you for causing me pain
I forgive you for bringing me bane
I forgive you for all you have done
I release this hurt to be burned by the sun
No more will you control my feelings
From right now I start my healings

Guidance Chant

I ask the universe to guide me right
To lead me to a whole new light
Show me the way, I ask of you
Show me what I need to view

Love Chant

Venus O' beautiful Goddess, guide the way of love to me
Aphrodite O' great Goddess, show the way of love to me
Cupid O' great God, I ask you shoot me with your arrow of love
Eros O' great God, shoot me with your arrow of love

Protection Chant

Goddess of all that's good and great
Give me protection, I give you my fate
God of light and all the land
Shield me from harm wherever I stand
Elements combine and circle me
Protect me from bad and let me be free

New Home Chant

Lord and lady bless this dwelling
Bad and negative energy I am expelling
I ask for love, happiness and success to fill these walls
Every day - and when night falls
Bad or harmful go away
I claim this house, I am here to stay

Sleep Chant

Goddess above, queen of the night
Help me sleep in your healing light
Restful sleep, come to me,
Relax my body, let my mind be free
Grant me calm and peace tonight
And let me wake in the Gods golden light

"White magic is entirely positive and harms no one, but seeks only to bring good things into your lives, to those we love and into the world"

Cassandra Eason

Rituals and Spells

Rituals

There are many rituals carried out in Wicca. Covens will have their own specific ones, passed down through generations of witches, led by a High Priestess and a High Priest but with every coven member playing their part. And these of course will vary, depending on what path the coven has chosen to follow.

What follows are rituals you can perform on your own or with friends. Most rituals are performed after casting a circle (see page 77) and many like to shower or bathe beforehand, and wear ritual robes or even do them skyclad (naked). This is so outside negativity or outside influences do not interfere with your workings. Rituals and Spells may seem the same but they are very different. A ritual is performed as part of the religion; it is not for gain or prosperity but something almost all Wiccans do to bring us closer to the divine. Spell work is something we do to gain or to bring something to us.

Smudging

Smudging is an ancient ritual to cleanse a space of negativity. Places and houses can be filled with negative or stale energies, or even bad spirits. Smudging will cleanse the space and make it pure. Many people use smudging when they move into a new house or if they feel that something isn't right about a place. You can also smudge around your altar before doing spell work or meditation. Make smudge sticks by drying out the herb you wish to use and then using paper (newspaper is best). Wrap it into a tight bundle, tie it together with string and leave for a few days. When the herbs have taken a cigar shape, tie them together with cotton, wool or thread. You can also buy smudge sticks from a metaphysical store relatively cheaply. The most common herb to use in smudging is sage, a renowned herb throughout the world for thousands of years. Sweetgrass is also used to bring harmony to a space. Use sage to dispel negative energy and sweetgrass to attract positive energy, while cedar, a protective herb, can be added to a smudge stick to give it extra power.

When you do the smudging open up all your doors and windows and light the stick. Let the smoke blow over yourself, then walk around the whole space of your home or wherever you are doing the ceremony and allow the smoke to drift in every little corner, in cupboards, lofts, basements, indeed everywhere. As you walk around with the smudge stick say something to empower the ritual, such as:

Cleanse this space, remove the past
Help me find happiness at long last
Fill this space with joy and love
Send your blessing from above

Making Holy Water

Holy water is used as a purification tool. It can be splashed around yourself or a home to bring peace and to dispel bad energy, and you can bless your altar tools and yourself with it. Making holy water is best done on a full moon. Pour water into a bowl and add some sea salt (alternatively use sea water).

Now hold your hands over the water and say:

I bless this water
May all negativity and impurities be dispelled
Goddess please bless this water
I exorcise this blessed water
So mote it be

Now put a finger in the water and make a clockwise circle motion three times around the bowl and say:

I consecrate this water in the name of the divine Goddess
May everything this water touch be blessed with purity and peace
So mote it be

To increase the water's power, leave it under the moonlight for a few hours and then bottle it. You may find you go through it quite fast, so it may become a monthly practice to make holy water every full moon.

Drawing Down The Moon

Drawing down the Moon is the act of inviting the divine awesome power of the Goddess into your very being. A very important practice, it will recharge your psychic energy and magic as well as bringing you closer to the divine Goddess. If you are in a coven this ritual will be carried out by the High Priestess when she takes the Goddess directly into her, but if you are a solitary witch you can perform this yourself.

Stand at your altar or outside, facing a full moon, with your arms crossed over your chest and your feet together. Now say:

Mother Goddess, lend me your light
Give me your power on this faithful night
I invoke you into my being and soul
Fill up my vessel and make me feel whole
I stand before you in awe and in love
I cherish your gifts you stow from above
I ask you tonight to show unto me
My Mother, My Goddess so mote it be

Now move your feet apart to about shoulder width, raise your arms up, stretch them out and welcome the Goddess to come into you. Close your eyes and feel the power of the moon's glow flow through you. Think about the power of the universe too, and what you are bringing into yourself. Stand for as long as you feel you need to, until you feel full with energy and that you have entered an altered state of consciousness. This is you being possessed by the divine, drawing the Goddess right into your soul. After you have performed this ritual you will be able to feel the Goddess inside you for some time afterwards. You may also feel an overwhelming sense of emotions while doing this ritual; it is not uncommon to cry or laugh hysterically.

Calling the Gods for Help

We call the Gods when we wish them to help us. Light a small fire in an open area, or alternatively light a black candle, before saying:

I call to the Gods, please hear my voice
I am in need I have no choice
Almighty Gods with many names
Come unto me beyond these flames
I ask of you for help this day
To come to me, to show me the way
Your strength and love know no bounds
Your truth and honour always astounds
I love you O' Gods I beckon on thee
Give me a sign and help me to see

Calling the Goddesses for Help

Calling the Goddesses is for when we need help and guidance from the Goddesses. Make a small fire or light a white candle and say:

O' Gracious Goddesses as ancient as time
Grant me your presence, give me a sign
The lady who is known by many a name
Please come to me by the power of flame
I ask for your help on this very night
To show me a way out of this plight
Most powerful queen who gave birth to all
Please watch over me, please hear my call

The Ancient Call

This is a chant to call on the ancients, which you can do on your own or as part of a group. Before starting the chant light a black candle to represent the God and a white candle to represent the Goddess. This will empower you before you do any spell work. Usually said on nights of a full moon or on a Sabbat, it is mostly used within Gardnerian Wicca. Eko is said to translate as 'hail' or 'hail and come forth.'

Eko, Eko, Azarak
Eko, Eko, Zamilak
Eko, Eko, Cernunnos
Eko, Eko, Aradia

Eko, Eko, Azarak
Eko, Eko, Zamilak
Eko, Eko, Cernunnos
Eko, Eko, Aradia

Eko, Eko, Azarak
Eko, Eko, Zamilak
Eko, Eko, Cernunnos
Eko, Eko, Aradia

Bagabi laca bachabe
Lamac cahi achababe
Karelyos!
Lmaca lamac bachalyos
Cabahagi sabalyos
Baryolas!
Lagoz atha cabyolas
Samahac atha famyolas
Hurrahya!

136

Charge of The God

Charge of the God is something you can do to feel closer to the Gods, if you need to be in their presence or convene with them, or if you wish to make offerings.

Cast a circle around your altar and call upon the elements. Light incense to cleanse the space and a black candle to represent the God, before reading out the following:

Listen to the words of the Great Father, who of old was called Osiris, Adonis, Zeus, Thor, Pan, Cernunnos, Herne, Lugh and by many other name:

"My Law is Harmony with all things
Mine is the secret that opens the gates of life
and mine is the dish of salt of the earth, that is the body of Cernunnos,
that is the eternal circle of rebirth.
I give the knowledge of life everlasting, and beyond death
I give the promise of regeneration and renewal.
I am the sacrifice, the father of all things,
and my protection blanket is the earth"

Hear the words of the dancing God, the music of whose laughter stirs the winds,

whose voice calls the seasons:

"I who am the Lord of the Hunt and the Power of the Light,
sun among the clouds and the secret of the flame,
I call upon your bodies to arise and come unto me.
For I am the flesh of the earth and all its beings.
Through me all things must die and with me are reborn.
Let my worship be in the body that sings,
for behold all acts of willing sacrifice are my rituals.
Let there be desire and fear, anger and weakness,
joy and peace, awe and longing within you.
For these too are part of the mysteries found within yourself, within me.
All beginnings have endings, and all endings have beginnings."
So Mote It Be!

Listen to the words of the Horned God, The Guardian of all things wild and free, and Keeper of the Gates of Death, whose call all must answer:

"I am the fire within your heart, the yearning of your Soul.
I am the Hunter of Knowledge and the Seeker of the Holy Quest;

137

I who stand in the darkness of light;
I am He whom you have called Death.

I am the Consort and Mate of Her we adore, call forth to me
Heed my call beloved ones,
come unto me and learn the secrets of death and peace.
I am the corn at harvest and the fruit on the trees.
I am He who leads you home.
Scourge and Flame, Blade and Blood,
these are mine and gifts to thee

Call unto me in the forest wild and on hilltop bare
and seek me in the Darkness Bright.
I who have been called Pan, Herne, Osiris, and Hades,
speak to thee in thy search.
Come dance and sing; come live and smile,
for behold: this is my worship
You are my children and I am thy Father.
On swift night wings
it is I who lay you at the Mother's feet
to be reborn and to return again
Thou who thinks to seek me,
know that I am the untamed wind,
the fury of storm and passion in your soul.
Seek me with pride and humility,
but seek me best with love and strength.
For this is my path,
and I love not the weak and fearful.
Hear my call on long winter nights
and we shall stand together
guarding Her Earth as She sleeps

I am the radiant King of the Heavens
flooding the Earth with warmth and encouraging the hidden
seed of creation to burst forth into manifestation
I lift my shining spear to light the lives of all beings
and daily pour forth my golden rays upon the Earth
putting to flight the powers of darkness

I am the spirit of all beasts wild and free.
I run with the stag and soar as a sacred falcon against
the shimmering sky

The ancient woods and wild places emanate my powers
the birds of the air sing of my sanctity

I am the harvest, offering up grain and fruits beneath
the sickle of time so that all may be nourished
For without planting there can be no harvest
without winter there can be no spring.

I am the thousand named Son of creation
Know that by all names I am the same

The spirit of the horned stag in the wild, the endless harvest
See in the yearly cycle of festivals my birth, death and
rebirth and know that such is the destiny of all creation

I am the spark of life, the radiant Sun, the giver of peace and rest
I send my rays of blessings to warm the hearts
and strengthen the minds of all

I am the fire within your heart,
the yearning hunger within your soul.
I am the Horned God,
the hunter of beasts and pursuer of the fare of knowledge.
I take up the sacred quest and see it to the end.

I, who stands within the darkness of light, am He who you call death.
But I am also the spark of life, the joy of existence,
the mirth in laughter, the shine across thine eyes.
I am the consort, mate, and son of She whom we adore.
I am the fruit upon the trees, the grain at harvest,
He who offers himself up so others may live.
I am He who leads you home.
Strength and flame, heart and humor, life and death,
these are my gifts unto thee.
Call upon me in the forest wild and on the hilltop bare
and seek me in darkness bright.

I am He who has been called Pan, Herne, Dianus,
Osiris, Apollo, Lugh, Dionysus,
and by many other names,
and I call to thee.
Come, dance and sing with the Lord of the Winds;

come, laugh and love with the SunKing,
for these are my worship.
On gliding night wings it is I who lay you at the Mothers feet
to be reborn and return again.
I too lay within her womb, planted in summer seed
to live on after my wintery death.
I am the untamed wind, the raging river,
the ocean crashing on the rocks,
the fury of the storm and the passion in your heart.
Seek me with courage or you will be swept away in your seeking.

Seek me with pride and humility,
but seek me best of all with love and strength
for this is my path.
Walk it with purpose and dance boldly.
Hear my call on long nights
and we shall stand together as one."

Charge of The Goddess

Charge of the Goddess is a ritual you can do to convene with the Goddess, to call her for advice and make offerings. Start by casting a circle and calling the elements. Light incense to cleanse your altar and a white candle to represent the Goddess, before reading the following:

Listen to the words of the Great Mother,
who was of old also called Artemis; Astarte; Diana;
Melusine; Aphrodite; Cerridwen; Dana;
Arianrhod; Isis; Bride;
and by many other names.

Whenever ye have need of anything,
once in a month,
and better it be when the Moon be full,
then ye shall assemble in some secret place
and adore the spirit of me,
who am Queen of all Witcheries.

There shall ye assemble,
ye who are fain to learn all sorcery,

140

yet have not yet won its deepest secrets:
to these will I teach things that are yet unknown.
And ye shall be free from slavery;
and as a sign that ye are really free,
ye shall be naked in your rites;
and ye shall dance, sing, feast,
make music and love, all in my praise.

For mine is the ecstasy of the spirit
and mine also is joy on earth;
for my Law is Love unto all beings.
Keep pure your highest ideal; strive ever toward it;
let naught stop you or turn you aside.
For mine is the secret door which opens upon the Land of Youth;
and mine is the Cup of the Wine of Life,
and the Cauldron of Cerridwen,
which is the Holy Grail of Immortality.

I am the Gracious Goddess,
who gives the gift of joy unto the heart.
Upon earth, I give the knowledge of the spirit eternal;
and beyond death, I give peace, and freedom,
and reunion with those who have gone before.
Nor do I demand sacrifice,
for behold I am the Mother of All Living,
and my love is poured out upon the earth.
Hear ye the words of the Star Goddess,
she in the dust of whose feet are the hosts of heaven;
whose body encircleth the Universe;

I, who am the beauty of the green earth,
and the white Moon among the stars,
and the mystery of the waters, and the heart's desire,
call unto thy soul.
Arise and come unto me.
For I am the Soul of Nature, who giveth life to the universe;
from me all things proceed, and unto me must all things return;
and before my face, beloved of gods and mortals,

141

thine inmost divine self
shall be unfolded in the rapture of infinite joy.

Let my worship be within the heart that rejoiceth
for behold:
all acts of love and pleasure are my rituals.
And therefore let there be beauty and strength,
power and compassion, honour and humility,
mirth and reverence within you.
And thou who thinkest to seek for me,
know thy seeking and yearning shall avail thee not,
unless thou know this mystery:
that if that which thou seekest thou findest
not within thee, thou wilt never find it without thee.

For behold, I have been with thee from the beginning;
and I am that which is attained at the end of desire.

Full Moon Cleansing Ritual

On the full moon we charge ourselves with the psychic energy of the Goddess. You can do this simply to meditate at your altar and let the energy enter you, but many Wiccans like to charge their tools and crystals under the moon's light too.

Cast your circle and sit at your altar. Have all your tools or talismans you wish to charge with psychic energy ready. Place them on your altar and say:

By the Goddess light, please charge my tools tonight
Cleanse them well with your love and grace
Bring your light to this place

Now wrap your tools in a cloth and place them where the moonlight can touch them, which could be on a windowsill or in your garden if it is safe to do so. Don't worry if the sky is clouded over because the moon's light is still present. Now close the circle and thank the Goddess, leaving a gift of gratitude if you wish to do so.

Spells

For most, casting spells is an essential part of being Wiccan, using, as it does, the power of nature and the elements to send a message to the universe in order to change or manipulate our futures or ask for something we want. Spell casting works best when the spells come from within you and are your own creation. I have given you the tools in this book in order to cast your own spells by using crystals, stones, colours, oils, candles and herbs. Below I have listed some very common spells used by Wiccans, tried and tested spells that have endured the test of time. Remember, if you use a God or Goddess or the Fae in your spell work, give them an offering as thanks, especially if the spell gives you what you wanted. The amount of spells you can do is totally up to you; just try not to be greedy and remember the laws of karma. Don't use spells to hurt anyone or mess with someone's will and you will be fine. Don't be scared to experiment with spells and have fun with them either. Casting spells is one of the greatest aspects of Wicca; it is the craft in witchcraft; it is who we are. Use magic everyday it brings us closer to the Gods and Goddesses.

The Witch's Bottle

Every witch should have a witch's bottle to prevent any negativity and ill will sent their way. Used to stop curses and hexes and prevent anyone doing us harm using magic, witch's bottles have been used since ancient times all over Europe and especially within Britain. Many houses in England that are more than three centuries old will have a witch's bottle buried somewhere within them. In fact they regularly turn up when a house is being demolished or renovated and there are over two hundred in museums. The most popular places to hide witch bottles used to be under the hearthstone or doorstep. Not only were these spots the least likely to be disturbed in a peasant cottage, but they were also the main openings by which a hostile spell might enter. Bottles were also plastered into walls, hidden in attics and buried in gardens or lonely places.

In the seventeenth and eighteenth centuries witch bottles often had faces stamped on the glass or stoneware. In Germany and the Low Countries they were called Bellarmine jars after the unpopular 16th century cardinal who first appeared on them in the Netherlands. The attraction of having a face on the bottle was that it would help trick a hostile spell or wish into thinking it had found its target and then get trapped inside, as in a rat-trap. These bottles were also popularly used for burying money, with spells cast on them to deflect treasure-hunters.

And so, the idea of a witch bottle is that it will attract and trap hostile enchantments by tricking them into believing they have found their target, i.e. you. The principle is almost the same as with voodoo dolls, but with the reverse intent. The bottle is meant to represent you so some of your personal fluids have to go into it. In the old days this was most commonly urine, with which the bottle is half filled. Next add some hair and perhaps nail-clippings or even blood if you feel seriously threatened. Blood is of course the most potent substance of all that you could use for this kind of magic (which is why vampires are so keen on it!) but, judging by the old witch bottles that have been chemically analysed, our forebears do not seem to have considered it necessary. However, if you happen to cut yourself while preparing your bottle, well, it would be silly not to take advantage of it for some added potency. Between them your ingredients will create a potent decoy of you on the magical plane. These days you are unlikely to find a jar with a face on it, but you could maybe draw a simple face on a piece of wood and add it to the mix. Opinions are divided over whether you should include a photograph of yourself. Some say it adds strength to the spell, others that it makes no difference and a few warn that it is positively dangerous in case the bottle falls into the wrong hands. You'll have to make up your own mind on this.

The next ingredients you need are some snares to trap the hostility being directed against you. These can be thorns, bent pins or nails, barbed wire, fishhooks - anything sharp and snagging in fact. Plus you can add a tangled ball of sewing thread, which is apparently very effective too. This is all you need to make your self-protecting witch bottle. Some witches also add Deadly Nightshade and other potentially lethal herbs, and these are supposed to help if you know how to handle them safely, but are not essential.

Poppets

Poppets are small dolls or something created to look like a thing you want to work your magic on. Many shows on TV and other media show a poppet doll as a voodoo doll, but this is not the case; poppets have been used in Celtic ceremonies and in Europe for a very long time. In fact, this is where we get the term puppet.

Poppets are mainly used to manifest a desire to us, and in healing magic. Make a doll from material that represents a certain person, and then add something personal of theirs into the stuffing of the doll. If it is made for healing, then fill the doll full of healing herbs and say a spell and/or incantations over it. The way a poppet works is a 'like creates like' attitude; what is done to the doll will have a bearing on the person it represents. You can also make poppets of things you would like to manifest into your life, such as money or love, by creating the poppet out of spare materials you have sitting around the home and then simply cutting the shapes you want out in double, filling the poppet with cotton or materials, adding whichever herbs or crystals you want to help manifest the outcome, and then sewing the two pieces of material together. Whilst sewing, think about the outcome you want and light a coloured candle for the spell you are creating.

Hot Foot Powder

Hot Foot Powder is an equal mixture of sea or rock salt, cayenne powder and black pepper, and is used to keep a person who intends harm away from you. To make this add the three ingredients to a pestle and mortar or a grinder and crush them together, whilst saying:

> *Hot foot, hot foot, you are too close*
> *I make this powder to keep you away*
> *May your feet get hot when you're around me*
> *and may you not want to stay*

If the person you want to keep away comes to your home, add the powder while repeating the words over your front path and doorway. If it is someone you see at work or in a public place, put the powder in their usual path for getting towards you while repeating the words.

144

Four Thieves Vinegar

Four Thieves Vinegar is used for protection and healing. The story of the spell goes like this: a group of thieves were robbing the dead and the sick during a European plague outbreak. When they were caught, the authorities asked them how they could rob the houses of the plague ridden victims without becoming sick themselves. The thieves told the authorities about the concoction they had made. They offered to exchange their secret recipe, which had allowed them to commit the robberies without catching the disease, in exchange for leniency. Doctors who tested the ingredients could not find any reason why it was beneficial with regards to the plague, so the vinegar was heralded as witchcraft and instead of a cure or symptom reliever it was heralded as a spell, although actually, similar types of herbal vinegars have been used as medicine since the time of Hippocrates.

Early recipes for this vinegar called for a number of herbs to be added into a vinegar solution and left to steep for several days. The following vinegar recipe hung in the Museum of Paris in 1937, and is said to have been an original copy of the recipe posted on the walls of Marseilles during an episode of the plague:

Take three pints of strong white wine vinegar and add a handful each of wormwood, meadowsweet, wild marjoram and sage. Next, add fifty cloves, two ounces of campanula roots, two ounces of angelic, rosemary and horehound, three large measures of camphor and two whole garlic bulbs. Place the mixture in a container for fifteen days, strain and then bottle. Use by rubbing it on the hands, ears and temples from time to time to keep away ill health, bad luck and negativity.

Abracadabra Charm

Abracadabra is an ancient spell, worn as a lucky amulet. The word comes from ancient Aramaic and translates as 'I will create when I speak.' The spell is written as below:

To expel a person, negativity, bills, or anything you want to get rid of, write on the thing you want to get rid of like this and it should banish it from your life.

A B R A C A D A B R A

A B R A C A D A B R

A B R A C A D A B

A B R A C A D A

A B R A C A D

A B R A C A

A B R A C

A B R A

A B R

A B

A

To bring something to you, write on the thing you want, even if it is just a picture or a drawing you have done. Write it like below. You can also wear this as an amulet for luck and protection.

A

A B

A B R

A B R A

A B R A C

A B R A C A

A B R A C A D

A B R A C A D A

A B R A C A D A B

A B R A C A D A B R

A B R A C A D A B R A

Elemental Spell Ritual

The Elemental Spell Ritual is a spell you can cast to bring or expel something from your life. It is a relatively simple ritual. If you want to bring something into your life you should perform it on a waxing moon, but if your wish is to expel something from your life then you should perform it on a waning moon. You can perform it from any of the four elements. Ask yourself which element would suit best what you're trying to achieve (see page 51). Use the appropriate coloured ink and candle too, and then simply wait; you will usually see a result within one cycle of the moon.

Water

1. Fill a bowl with salted water - sea salt works best for this.

2. Get a small piece of paper and write down with the appropriate coloured pen or pencil what you want to happen, for example, love, a new job, money.

3. Get an appropriate coloured candle, light it and stand it over the bowl so the fire from the candle reflects into the water.

4. Place the paper into the water, push it down and give it a little shake around under the water.

5. Say "by the element of water, I ask you to come unto me and grant my desire."

6. Wait for the writing on the paper to fade or disappear altogether. If it doesn't fade then give it a little swirl around the bowl a few times.

7. Take the water with the paper, bury them inside the earth, close your eyes and say "this is my will so mote it be."

Fire

1. Fill a bowl with salted water – again, sea salt works best for this.

2. Get a small piece of paper and write down with the appropriate coloured pen or pencil what you want to happen, for example, love, a new job, money.

3. Get an appropriate coloured candle, light it and stand it over the bowl so the fire from the candle reflects into the water.

4. Light the paper with the candle and say, "by the power of fire, I ask that you let my desire manifest" and then let the ashes fall into the water.

5. Now take the water and the paper ashes and bury them into the earth and say "this is my will so mote it be."

Air

1. Light an appropriate coloured candle.

2. Write down on a small piece of paper what it is you want, with the appropriate coloured pen or pencil.

3. Now say, "by the power of air I ask that you let my desire manifest."

4. Take the candle and the paper to a window or a door that leads outside, and wait for the candle to blow out naturally.

5. When the candle has blown out, take the paper you wrote on and let the wind take it from you hand saying "this is my will so mote it be."

Earth

1. Light an appropriate coloured candle outdoors, you may need to shield it from the wind.

2. Using the appropriately coloured pen or pencil, write your desire on a small piece of paper.

3. Dig a small hole in the ground and say, "I ask the power of earth to manifest my desire."

4. Put the paper in the hole and bury it, then let a few drops of the candlewax fall on top of the place where you buried the paper. Say "this is my will so mote it be."

War Water

War Water is a very old spell, also known as Mars water. It is based on the metal iron which is the metal of Mars, the God of War. If you have an enemy or someone who is harassing you or making you feel intimidated or uncomfortable, you can use war water. But remember the harm none rule; if you use this against innocent people it will backfire on you.

To do this spell you need to collect iron such as iron nails, place them in water and put the water with the iron in your refrigerator. Cut the iron first to make sure it rusts. Keep opening the jar once or twice a day to let air into the jar to encourage the rust. After about two weeks, when the water is a reddish colour from the rust, drain the water into a small jar or bottle. Now take the water and think of the bad things your enemy has done to you, and pour the water on their driveway, or wall of their house. Now every time they do something bad to you it will bounce back onto them.

To Reverse a Spell

You will need a black candle, some oil, some salt, and a sage smudge stick.

Rub the black candle with oil, but do this by starting at the top and rubbing down to the bottom, all the while thinking deeply about the spell(s) you want to break, Put a circle of salt around the bottom of the black candle then light it, now with the candle flame light the sage smudge stick and move around the table you have the candle on in an anti-clockwise direction and say:

> *The spell I cast, make it no longer last*
> *I want to reverse to how it was before*
> *I do not want this spell anymore*

Now start walking around the table in a clockwise direction and say:

> *The spell is now broken*
> *I have awoken*
> *After the candle light burns out*
> *So will the spell I cast in doubt.*
> *So mote it be*

Let the black candle burn itself out. When it has, gather the salt and the candle and bury them. Any spells you have done since the last full moon, which you thought about here, will be cancelled out.

The Rainbow Spell

A rainbow is the entire spectrum of colours of visible light. There is much magic in rainbows, while some simply feel that seeing a rainbow is lucky. And this spell does bring you luck - in anything; from love and money to protection and happiness.

You need seven coloured candles; red, orange, yellow, green, blue, indigo and violet.

Get a pot or a bowl for you to melt wax into. Then, on the day of a new moon, light the red candle inside the bowl and say 'I call on the power of the rainbow to colour my life and to end my strife.' Let the candle burn itself out. If you're not watching it make sure it is somewhere safe where it won't catch fire. Do not remove any melted wax.

On the second day melt a little of the red wax and stand the orange candle in the melted red wax. Light the orange candle and say 'I call on the power of the rainbow to colour my life and to end my strife,' and then let the orange candle burn down.

Do this each day for seven days until you have used all the candles, in this particular order: red, orange, yellow, green, blue, indigo and violet. Take the mixed coloured wax (warm the bowl a little to remove the wax) and then bury it in the earth and say 'I call on the power of the rainbow with these colours I hold, please grant me your fabled pot of gold'

By the time of the full moon, you should find that things are looking up for you.

Florida Water

Florida in Spanish means flower, so this really means flower water and is used for cleansing. Scrub your altar and tools with it to remove negative influences Use it as an after bath to remove any negativity, or as cologne for spiritual services, protection, good luck and purifications. It can also be used as a cooling wash to aid headaches or simply as a lovely perfume. When someone throws something in your yard or gives you something you feel is cursed, immediately sprinkle it with Florida Water. You can also use it as an offering to the Gods and your ancestors.

What you need:

5 cups of vodka

3 cups of rose petals

3 cups of jasmine flowers

3 cups of aromatic greens, such as mint, lemon balm, lemon verbena, basil, rosemary, peppermint, thyme etc

3 cinnamon sticks

1 whole orange with peel, chopped up

1 whole lemon with peel, chopped up

1 whole grapefruit with peel, chopped up

Mix these ingredients on a new moon and leave to ferment for one whole lunar cycle. On the following new moon, strain the water using a sieve. Keep it in a glass jar or bottle and use as and when you wish to. You can use essential oils instead of roses and jasmine flowers, but you will only need a few drops of each. And you can change other ingredients to suit.

Love Spell 1

On a new moon, fill a bath and add rose petals or rose essential oil. Light four pink candles and put them on the four corners of your bath. While you lie in the bath think about love, think about how it will make you feel and how it will change your life. Think about your perfect partner and what you would like. Welcome love into your life. Invite it in. For the next two weeks wear something with vanilla in it; this can be a vanilla scented perfume or deodorant, vanilla essential oil, or even a couple of vanilla pods carried around with you. Love should show itself by the time of the full moon.

Love Spell 2

Take three cords or strings of various pleasing pastel colours and braid them tightly together. Firmly tie a knot near one end of the braid, thinking of your need for love. Next, tie another knot, and another, until you have tied seven knots. Wear or carry the cord with you until you find your love.

Witches Ladder

The Witches Ladder is a powerful spell that can be used to create anything you wish for.

What you need:

Wool, lace or ribbon

A length of red cord

A length of white cord

A length of black cord

7 feathers

This is best done on a full moon. Tie the top of the three cords together. Now braid them while saying

Yarn of red, black and white

Work your magic spell this night

Say this until you have braided all the pieces together and then tie a knot at the bottom.

Now take a feather and say what it is you wish for, and then tie the feather with a knot onto the braided length of cord and say your wish while you are doing this. When it is done say

With this feather and this string

Prosperity this charm will bring

Now repeat for all of the other six feathers.

You can do this spell for luck using seven different coloured feathers; red for physical vitality; blue for mental abilities, peace and protection; yellow for cheerfulness and prosperity; green for growth and health; brown for stability and respect; black for mystical wisdom; iridescent black for mystical sight and barred black, grey or white for balance and harmony. Feathers with eyes such as peacock feathers can be used for protection and inner clairvoyant vision.

Now hang your witches ladder in your home and it will act as a charm for whatever it is you asked for.

Money Spell

Money Spells come in all shapes and sizes, but I have found this one to work best and it is so easy to do. Take a penny or the lowest monetary denomination of your country and hold it in your hand. Now put the penny on your third eye (between your eyes) and imagine having money to spare, a good bank balance or a pocket full of cash. Now take the penny to a body of water and say

Prosperity, riches and good fortune I beckon

I call to the Gods of good fortune

To help me in my hour of need

May this penny grow

As the oak grows from seed

If you do get a windfall or some money from the spell, make sure to thank the gods and leave them a gift of gratitude. Alternatively, you can give a little of the money to a good cause or someone in need to keep your karma in balance.

Protection Spell

There are many herbs, stones and crystals that offer amazing protective qualities, and just carrying these around with you will absorb and disperse negative energies. See the relevant chapters for further information.

Charm Bags

Charm bags are basically just spells in a bag; you can add as many items as you like into a little pouch or sachet to carry around with you or to hang around your home, car or place of work. You can fill them with herbs, stones, crystals, jewellery, special items from precious memories, money, metal, wood or anything else that helps make the charm personal and magical to you.

However, the colour of the bag is particularly important:

Gold: *wealth, protection, the God*

Silver: *prosperity, the moon, psychism, the Goddess*

White: *purity, all colours combined, the Goddess*

Yellow: *healing, finding employment*

Orange: *communication, messages, travel*

Green: *prosperity, abundance, friendship, growth, nature*

Blue: *peace, calm, wisdom, benevolence*

Purple: *wisdom, mysteries, wealth, grandeur, justice*

Red: *success, strength, romance, protection*

Pink: *love, friendship, healing*

Brown: *houses, home, justice, earth, permanence*

Black: *absorbs and dissolves baneful energy, the God*

"When a man is not concerned with seeing, things look
very much the same to him every time he looks at the world.
When he learns to see, on the other hand,
nothing is ever the same every time he sees it…"
Shaman don Juan Matan

Divination and Empaths

WHEEL of FORTUNE

Divination

Wiccans use a host of tools to predict or even change futures. Divination is a form of fortune telling or seeing into the future and has been around for thousands of years. Some Wiccans are born with a psychic ability and from a very young age have been extra sensitive to earth's vibrations. Psychics can read people, or feel differently about certain spaces they go to by picking up on these energies. They will often be able to see futures and pasts without even trying. To some this can be a blessing but to others it may be seen as a curse; not everyone wants this psychic ability thrust upon them. But even those who see it as a curse must admit it can be very helpful to have this ability sometimes.

However, in truth everyone has psychic ability and it can be exercised like a muscle and learned just as you can learn to write or do mathematics. And like most things, the more you do it, the better you become. However, if this is something you wish to develop in yourself, then it is essential you read much more deeply on whatever form of divination you are most interested in, as it is impossible to cover divination in any depth in an introductory book on Wicca. Scrying and using a pendulum are, however, two practises you could try straight away.

To put it as simple as possible, divination is opening yourself up to allow messages and signs to come to you. Psychic ability comes from your subconscious brain so in order to use your ability you must first learn to block everything out from your conscious brain. Your conscious brain deals with work, family, money and all your day to day dealings. It helps you focus, think and learn; whether that's riding a bike, tying your shoelaces as a child or reading a newspaper. It needs to be operating much of the time, and yet it only represents 10% of the total capacity of the human brain. The unconscious mind then, represents 90% of the human brain. It is the unconscious side that is operating when we are dreaming, or when memories float back to us. In fact, our unconscious mind stores all our memories and experiences, and even our futures. In divination, your subconscious must be allowed to take over so you forget about all your daily routines and worries and instead let your subconscious get to work. A great way to do this is through meditation, so please refer back to the chapter on that if you need to.

Below are some of the tools we use in Wicca to predict the future and see into the past.

Scrying

Scrying is the practice of looking into a reflective surface and being able to see things such as a spiritual sign, the answer to a question or the futures of yourself and others. Tools used in scrying are black mirrors (a plate of glass sprayed black on one side so it has a reflective surface) a crystal ball, a bowl of water with a candle flame reflected in it, a candle flame itself and a still body of water. When scrying try to relax your whole body and when staring into the reflective surface let your subconscious mind take over and let it show you what you need to see.

Tarot

Tarot cards are thousands of years old and so mysterious that no one actually knows where they came from or the date they came into being. We do know however, that people who used divination, including tarot, risked punishment by disapproving Christians in the middle ages. Thankfully, most of us live in a world that is not quite so cruel and tarot readings, as well as all other forms of pagan worship and beliefs, are enjoying their resurgence.

The Tarot is a set of seventy eight cards. In the deck are twenty two major arcana, the most important cards that have more meaning when pulled out in a reading, and fifty six minor arcana, made up of four suits - cups, pentacles, wands and swords. Each suit goes up to ten and then there is a page, knight, king and queen also. The whole pack of cards are sorted into different spreads which represent different aspects of life such as past, present, future. And they are read depending on which card comes up at which aspect it is within the spread.

Because the art of tarot reading is open to the skill and interpretation of the practitioner, and therefore can be very complicated to learn, I have opted to write only this brief introduction about tarot here. For those of you interested in learning the secrets and skills of tarot, I am writing a book that shows how easy, interesting and life-changing they can be to learn and use. I'm hoping this book will be published towards the end of 2014 or start of 2015.

Palmistry

Palmistry is an ancient form of divination and is the practice of reading the lines on a person's hand. Each line on your palm represents a different aspect of life, such as a marriage or a lifeline. Depending on the shape, length and deepness of each line, palmistry can tell much about the person and their future.

Rune Casting

Rune Stones were said to have been a gift from the Great God Odin. The word rune means 'whisper' or 'secret' and runes were used as an ancient language. Each symbol represents a letter and has a different meaning attributed to it, while together they make an alphabet. There are twenty four rune stones in the most commonly used set called the futhark. They are cast by taking a handful, throwing them down and reading the meaning. Like tarot, there can be different runic spreads. The twenty four runic signs are arranged into three families comprising eight runes each. These individual families are called Aett (singular) or Aettir (plural). Each family or Aett is ruled over by its own particular spirit or Norse God. Respectively these entities are Freya & Frey, Goddess and God of fertility and increase, Heindall, watcher and the keeper of the rainbow bridge to the heavens, and Tyr, war leader and spirit of the just. Every rune is also a magic talisman and can be worn for a number of different reasons. When different runes are put together to make a shape or symbol in picture form they are what is known as a sigil. Sigils are symbols that you can put on any number of things to give them magical meaning. You can carve sigils into candles, paint them on your walls, write them in chalk on the pavement, carve them into wood or scrape them in the dirt or sand.

Pendulum

Used for centuries to and most famous for telling the sex of a baby, pendulums can be anything with a weight on that is attached to a piece of string. You can buy expensive gold, silver or jewel encrusted pendulums or you can make one yourself. Pendulums are used by asking it a question and then watching which way it swings, but first you need to tune it into yourself. You start by saying 'please show me the answer for Yes' and then watch which way the pendulum swings. Then you need to tune it to a 'No' answer for you. Ask 'please show me the answer for No' and watch which way it swings for this. If it swings the same way as 'Yes' simply keep going, until it swings the other way. Then the pendulum will be in tune with your own rhythms and you will be ready to use it.

Empaths

Empaths are people who can feel others feelings, often mistaken as psychics because they just know stuff, without being told. It's a knowing that goes way beyond intuition or gut feelings, even though that is how many would describe the 'knowing.'

An empath can see a person's likes and hates, can feel their sadness and happiness, and can sometimes be overwhelmed with emotions when they walk into a room full of other people. They don't even have to be in the same room as others either, especially with loved ones, but from afar can still feel their pain and hurt or sadness and sense something is wrong.

An empath can also know instantly if someone is lying and being dishonest, or if someone means them harm, and instinctively knows if someone is a good or bad person. Some empaths can smell emotions or illness in others. Often they can become sad or depressed without understanding why. This is because they are absorbing negativity and others emotions from all around them. In fact they can even feel someone else's physical pain if they are hurt or unwell.

And so, perhaps quite understandably, empaths love to be in happy places, because just as much as they can feel negative emotions they can also feel happy ones too. Consequently, they love fun fairs, holidays with others, the spontaneity and joy of children, and listening to any happy news. It can be very hard to switch off if you're an empath, and you can feel drained much of the time and find it difficult to sleep. Empaths can also have a high dependency on alcohol or drug use because it stops the emotions of others seeping through and they can feel their own emotions more when high or drunk. They also love loud music as this can drown out unwanted thoughts. Escapism is a big must for most empaths as they can tire of taking on everyone else's problems and need a break, whether that be through movies, video games, drinking, drugs, music or even just throwing themselves into work or family life. When empaths do not have a release they will find themselves spending almost every moment doing things for others.

And for some, it can be really difficult to ensure they make time for themselves, because people are drawn to empaths as metal is to magnets, often because of the empaths warmth and openness. Empaths are very honest as well, perhaps sometimes too honest, but they are very open people and people find this a comfort because an empath knows just what to say as they know how the other person is feeling.

If you are an empath and finding things difficult…

Please be assured; there are lots of people like you who find it difficult to turn off emotionally because of all the other emotions going on all around. But you do need to take the bull by the horns and learn to live with it, because you cannot get rid of it and you cannot keep ignoring it.

Write a day to day diary of when the feelings start, when they are at their highest and when you feel most comfortable. What is the emotion you are feeling when you become drained or when you can't sleep? Is it sadness or grief? Is it fear? You need to start singling out emotions and when or why you are feeling them.

Try to centre yourself; this could be done through meditation or by your own technique. The goal is to learn how to turn off your empathy within a particular moment and to train yourself to do this by any means; however that feels right to you.

You have got to make a conscious choice to work hard every day on controlling it as otherwise it can start to control you, leaving you depressed and drained of energy. It is important you learn to shield yourself from negativity and emotions, for the sake of yourself and others.

Do a smudge of your home often, preferably with sage, and keep protective crystals with you such as onyx, lapis lazuli and tiger's eye. Try taking St John's wort as this will help take the edge off, but also be thankful that you are an empath, as when controlled this can be a great asset both for yourself and for others.

"We are born at a given moment, in a given place and, like vintage years of wine, we have the qualities of the year and of the season of which we are born"
Carl Jung

Sun Sign Astrology

Wiccan hold astrology as a very important part of our lives. We live by the seasons, the moon and the sun, and many of our Gods and Goddesses are named after the planets and constellations. Days and months are named after our deities, and time itself is dictated by the rising and setting of the sun. Astrology goes back as far as anyone can remember. It was studied by the Mayans, the Ancient Egyptians, the Chinese, Native Americans, Greeks, Romans, Babylonians, Norse and most other civilisations. And of course, it is still very much studied to this day.

The placing of the sun in the cosmos affects our emotions; it is good to bear this in mind on full moons and new moons. Throughout the year the sun and moon go through the twelve signs and the astrological zodiac and each one has a dramatic effect on us. It is easy to find out what sign the sun or moon is in at any given time; there are many websites and even phone apps that can tell you.

Your sun sign is fixed from the date you were born. This is the sign that gives you personality traits, with many born under the same zodiac signs having similar personality traits as you.

The moon moves through each zodiac sign on a monthly basis too, although these are not fixed. And so, when the moon moves into a new sign we take on personality traits of that sign. For example; if the moon was in Leo, we would be filled with energy and our ambitions would be high, but if the moon was in Pisces our emotions would be raw and we would be feeling very spiritual. We take the moon sign into consideration when doing any spell work or for rituals during an Esbat.

When giving people astrology signs on their day of birth, the ancients also took into consideration the seasons and other traits at the time of year. If your sign date is within a few days of another sign you may have personality traits of that sign too. This is called being 'on the cusp' of another sign. Your main sign though, will always be within the dates you were born. Professional astrologers can give you an excellent astrology reading if they know the exact date and time you were born. This is called a birth chart.

Additionally, each sign is attached to an element and takes on that element's personality. Earth signs are Taurus, Virgo and Capricorn. Very much 'in the now', they do not like nonsense and believe in what they can see touch and feel. Workers and money makers, earth signs are honest and dependable. People born under Taurus can be particularly stubborn and once they set their mind on something they become very passionate about it. Virgos like to be busy, paying a lot of attention to every small detail. Capricorns are organisers, can do a task repeatedly without getting bored and often do whatever needs to be done to work their way to the top.

Fire signs Aries, Leo and Sagittarius are often ambitious, competitive and hot headed. They don't like to sit around waiting for things to happen; they are go getters, and even though others can see fire signs as arrogant and self-centred they actually have the biggest and most generous hearts. Arians like to take control of situations while those born under the sign of Leo are artistic and creative and can be very competitive. Sagittarians thirst for knowledge and love to travel and explore.

Cancer, Scorpio and Pisces are water signs; emotional, intuitive and sometimes psychic. Water signs put great emphasis on the feelings of themselves and others. They are passionate and loving. Cancers hold onto anything with value and often want more in life than they have. Scorpions are natural born detectives and have very strong emotions, even if they don't always show them. Pisces have compassion for their fellow human beings, believing everyone should have equal rights and often fighting for them.

Gemini, Libra and Aquarius are all air signs that are sociable and deal with the intellect. Air signs often prefer to discuss things and talk about emotion rather than feel them. Those born under Gemini love to learn and talk about life and its bigger issues such as family, politics and topical news. In fact they often love to talk so much they need a constant flow of information or they feel left out of the loop. Librans like to communicate with their bodies and can be flirtatious. Passionate about justice and everyone's right to have a fair hearing, they gravitate towards family more than any other sign. Aquarians are very intelligent, like to be different and do things their own way, often crossing boundaries and with a very varied mix of friends.

Astrology can be so complex it is a whole science in itself. There are some very lengthy books and websites if you wish to delve deeper but always do your research and read reviews first. Below is a list of the different astrological signs and their personality traits.

Aries

The Ram, 21st March – 19th April

Element: Fire

Birthstone: Diamond

Tree: Alder

Planet: Mars

Arians are fire signs which mean they are often hot headed and do things quickly once they get an idea, with little patience for waiting around or pondering. This is not necessarily a negative aspect; Arians are quick thinkers and so the idea will often be well thought out and will work most of the time. Aries is a sign that likes to be in charge and you will often find an Arian as a boss or working their way to being the boss. They like to lead and are very sympathetic to others needs so are fair, but they do not like laziness or time wasters. However, Arians can be very critical and opinionated, even bullying without realising it, because they feel by voicing their opinion they are doing their best for the other person. Consequently, they can get into a lot of arguments. Quick to temper and often impatient, it would not be advised to rile an Aries or make them wait as this can make them furious, although they can be quick to cool down once an apology or a solution has been sought.

An Arian is a great friend to have as they are very loyal and generous. They are also good with finances, love a bargain and like to treat friends and make people smile. On the other hand, they like to be in the thick of things and do not appreciate being ignored. In fact they can be very nasty to someone who doesn't get on with them or who doesn't give them their attention and they are not shy in telling others why they have a problem with them.

Not the tidiest of people, they have no time for small boring day-to-day details, preferring the bigger picture instead. But they are organised in their affairs and like to keep appointments and pay their bills on time. An Arian needs structure in their lives. It is unthinkable to them that someone can look down on them for any reason, so they give them no reason to.

How to Love an Arian

Tell an Arian when they are doing something right to give them reassurance. They may act as if they don't need this but they do appreciate it. An Arian always seems confident and reassured but if you dig a bit deeper you will see that they are just as vulnerable as the rest of us. Never take an Arian's generous gestures for granted; make a point of it when they do something nice for you. Always show up when you say you will as Arians do not appreciate lateness or being stood up. Given they are strongly opinionated and love a good discussion you will have to be ready to debate with them, but try to make sure it doesn't turn into a full blown argument. You should be an adventurous lover and not let them get bored, as Arians like a spicy sex life.

Taurus

The Bull, 20th April – 20th May

Element: Earth

Birthstone: Emerald

Tree: Willow

Planet: Venus

Taureans are usually transparent; what you see is what you get. They are honest and hate dishonesty in others, which they can often spot very quickly. Taureans do not jump into action quickly but instead prefer to weigh up all pros and cons before making any decisions, and they will mostly go for safer options. After all, why take risks when there is no need?

Those born under the sign of Taurus love food and spoiling themselves and therefore should be careful as too much luxury can make them lazy and unhealthily overweight. However, they are one of the best workers you can meet and are excellent for getting a job done. Give

160

them a task and they will do it to the best of their ability, no matter how long or difficult it is. They have no patience for people who moan and whine about a task though and can dislike negative people as Taureans try to always stay positive. Taurean memory is usually excellent too; you rarely see them taking notes or writing lists as they can remember everything. Show them a task once and they can often do it straight away.

Taureans are often brilliant at making money and also excellent at spending it. They can be thought of as rather frivolous but they do love to save money too, and this comes from a deep need for security; they can feel very uncomfortable if they have no money in the bank. As they're blessed with a methodical mind that can see solutions to problems very easily, people often go to Taureans for advice. In many instances Taureans prefer to work alone though as others often don't match their work ethic. They enjoy their own company, but this doesn't mean they are loners as they also love parties and social gatherings, especially if there is plenty of alcohol and food on offer.

How to love a Taurean

Taureans can be very insecure and jealous so you may need to show them you are loyal to ensure they are comfortable with you. It's sometimes best to let a Taurean win an argument, even if you know you are right; they can be very passionate and stubborn about certain subjects and will argue and argue until they grind you down. Taureans love luxury and beautiful things, so if you are going to buy them a gift try and make it beautiful. Sexually a Taurean often needs to be led as they are not too forward romantically, although they are very sensual lovers once aroused.

Gemini

The Twins, 20th May – 21st June

Element: Air

Birthstone: Pearl

Tree: Hawthorn

Planet: Mercury.

Geminis must always be doing something or have something they are saving for or looking forward to or they can become restless or depressed. Naturally clever both in life and in education, they are very inquisitive and hate not knowing something, especially from friends and family. They love to laugh and play pranks and practical jokes, but they do not enjoy having the joke played on them, which stems from their frustration about being kept in the dark about things.

Geminis are very loving and often have a lot of friends, but they can be flighty, skipping from here to there, and so it can often be difficult to get hold of them. But don't worry; a Gemini will seek you out, and they will be full of wondrous stories and gossip and have a good catch up from when they last saw you.

Geminis are also ambitious and excellent workers, doing best in jobs that require communication. They make excellent sales representatives because their talk and friendly trusting nature means people instantly like them. Often on the telephone or sending texts, or arranging to meet up with new and old friends, they can think everyone is desperate to hear their news or what they've been doing since you last talked.

You don't see many single Geminis and if you do they are often not single for a prolonged period of time as they need to be in a relationship. Usually loyal and loving, if a relationship doesn't work Geminis won't mope over it for too long but will quickly move onto the next one.

How to love a Gemini

To love a Gemini you must be ready to deal with their personality which can vary from hour to hour. They may start a task, get bored and move onto something else quickly, and if they are not stimulated intellectually they can become very irritable. Frustratingly for others, they may talk all the way through a movie if it isn't something that is educating them. You also must enjoy talking and having long conversations, but above all you must have a good sense of humour. Geminis are good lovers and like to experiment; there isn't anything they won't try. You will never get bored with a Gemini lover.

Cancer

The Crab, 21st June – 22nd July

Element: Water

Birthstone: Ruby

Tree: Oak

Planet: The Moon

Cancerians appear tough on the outside but are actually very sensitive and loving and you are a special person if they show you their soft side. A Cancerian loves their home and spends time making it just the way they want it, as it's a place they go to heal and feel comfortable. They love anything old or with a history such as museums, antiques and thrift shops and also get on very well with the elderly as they value their experiences and wisdom. The cancer sign can worry a lot though and do need to learn to relax at times.

Cancerians like to hide things and do love to keep things for themselves. This doesn't necessarily mean they are greedy or selfish however; in fact the things they hide may only be of sentimental value and to you or I may be trivial, but to Cancerians such things are gold. Many Cancerians do hate to part with money though and are connoisseurs of bagging a bargain. A very caring sign, they often work in caring professions and are excellent listeners and problem solvers. They can make brilliant sales people if there is an advisory aspect to it, and a significant number of teachers are born under the sign of Cancer.

How to love a Cancerian

Cancerians enjoy the company of others and love talking about the past, but you must allow them to tell you in their own time as they do not like to be questioned. However, they do enjoy teaching and answering questions that are educational or work related. Always speak the truth to a Cancerian because if they sense dishonesty they're likely to leave. Let them know if you're in it for the long haul and don't dwell on their flaws but instead try to be optimistic. Cancerians are sensual lovers and love to touch and caress, they enjoy foreplay and kissing.

Leo

The Lion, 23rd July – 22nd August

Element: Fire

Birthstone: Onyx

Tree: Holly

Planet: The Sun

Leos are always right; or rather they think they are. However they do have an unbelievable knack for knowing what to do at the right time, which does make them excellent leaders. They also have a wide knowledge that somehow comes naturally; even they couldn't tell you how they know most of the stuff they know. Their brains are like sponges, soaking up information from everywhere. Perhaps understandably, Leos are very competitive and don't appreciate losing or being second best. But they are also positive and see no sense in being down, preferring to laugh and joke. They have high standards for themselves internally and externally and you will rarely see a Leo looking drab and shabby.

Leos excel at work; no matter what job they do they will always do it to the best of their abilities and, being Leos, they feel the place would fall apart if it were not for them being there. And when they are not sleeping then they are almost always doing some kind of activity as they struggle to sit still and do nothing. Leos are usually very popular as they are very generous, friendly and helpful with everyone they meet, but they can have a tendency to be two-faced and be nice to someone but despise them behind their back. They love sleeping and can from time to time become rather lazy, but this rarely lasts long because as soon as they recoup their energy they are back on the go again with their boundless energy.

How to love a Leo

Leos need to lead in a relationship and feel that they are in charge. If they feel undermined or taken for granted they may leave. Never try to trap a Leo because they need to feel free to pursue their dreams, but don't worry - they are very loyal once they are in a safe and loving relationship. Always try to be positive because they hate negativity. Compliment them frequently and they will love it. Leos are excellent lovers and enjoy long energetic sex.

Virgo

The Virgin, 23rd August- 22nd September

Element: Earth

Birthstone: Sapphire

Tree: Hazel

Planet: Mercury

Virgos seek perfection and can be fussy and critical because they are looking for everything to be just right. And as Virgo is the sign of cleanliness they can't live or be in unsanitary places. They may be a little messy, leaving clothes and papers lying about, but they are never dirty.

Virgos are also very inquisitive and have a need to always know what is going on. Indeed they will have a network of friends they talk to often so they are never left out of the loop. Virgos find it hard to relax though, and when they are relaxing or simply not doing anything they often see it as time wasted. Excellent friends if you're ever in trouble or have a crisis, a Virgo is the one to call as they can often have the problem sorted in seconds. Virgos are excellent workers too, in any number of jobs, and even repetitive or hard working jobs that other signs couldn't or wouldn't do. They have a down to earth work ethic to get a job done and done well.

How to love a Virgo

Virgos do not easily allow their emotions to be shown so respect this and don't push them for romance and flowers. Let them do things in their own way and let them keep their routines, even if they don't make much sense to you. Appreciate a Virgo's helpfulness and congratulate them on a job well done. Virgos may be pernickety about little things and may never seem satisfied but they do make wonderful lovers in the bedroom when they feel comfortable and relaxed and are able to let their emotional wall down.

Libra

The Scales, 23rd September – 22nd October

Element: Air

Birthstone: Opal

Tree: Ivy

Planet: Venus

Librans love to love and can become very depressed if they feel unwanted or unloved. Family is the most important thing to a Libran and they will do anything for their family and friends. However, they often find it difficult to make decisions because they see things from both sides by weighing up the pros and cons, thus struggling to come to a conclusion. Usually then, they are happy to just go with the flow. Librans love to entertain and have company and sometimes struggle with being alone so will often have friends over. They also love food, going out to eat and drink and spending money so it's not unusual to see them counting the pennies or dieting.

In work Librans are great with others and can get along with just about anyone, so any jobs that involve working with people or members of the public will suit a Libran. Rarely out of their comfort zone and happy in the same job for many years, Librans are helpful and friendly and may seem soft and easy to people they meet, but don't let this fool you as they can actually be very tough.

How to love a Libran

Librans are often very beautiful but they lack confidence so give them a boost and they will hugely appreciate it. They love the outdoors and nature so go for long walks into the countryside or along the beach. And if taking a Libran on a date they love rich and indulgent food so would be very happy to go to a good restaurant. As they can see two sides of everything and are great debaters they love to debate issues and enjoy long discussions on topical issues. And when they feel they can let go with someone they make erotic and sensual lovers.

Scorpio

The Scorpion, 23rd October – 21st November

Element: Water

Birthstone: Topaz

Tree: Reed

Planet: Pluto

Never short of admirers, Scorpios radiate beauty and have a wonderful sense of humour, loving to laugh. They also have a very sharp brain and can often remember information or come up with ideas immediately so it's best to avoid arguing with a Scorpio. And just like their symbol, the scorpion, they have a nasty sting and take no prisoners. Scorpios like to be in charge in their life, often dominating the homestead, but they are very loving and generous and make loyal and helpful friends if you are kind to them. Just don't give a Scorpio a reason to dislike you as they can hold grudges for a very long time. They can also be particularly jealous, always trying to keep up appearances, and if someone has more or better than they have they may think that person is arrogant or boastful. Naturally inquisitive, they need to know everything, making great lawyers, police officers and private detectives, or indeed any job that entails retrieving information with their natural knack for getting to the truth.

How to love a Scorpio

If you make a Scorpio look good in public they will love you for it. They like to keep up appearances so anything you can do to enhance them publicly will make them your friend. Scorpios like you to do little things for them to show you're thinking of them; just simple gestures such as texting them while at work or giving them a thoughtful gift. And make sure you listen to a Scorpio when they say they need time alone as they can have a bad temper so sometimes need space to cool off.

Sagittarius

The Archer, 22nd November – 21st December

Element: Fire

Birthstone: Turquoise

Tree: Elder

Planet: Jupiter

Sagittarians are the most open of all the signs and don't usually hold anything back; everyone knows what a Sagittarian is up to because they tell everyone. You will rarely see a Sagittarian telling lies because they are very honest and open, and although they may seem nasty at times, this is actually part of their honesty and they are just speaking what they feel is the truth. Of course this can seem hurtful to some, but many admire Sagittarius honesty because it means they know where they stand. Sagittarians love to travel and experience new things and often have the most diverse set of friends from all walks of life. Funny and quick witted, they make excellent stand-up comedians, entertainers and speakers. And although they are natural money makers, they rarely have it for long as they also love to spend money. In work Sagittarians often flit from one job to the next as they find it hard to settle on one thing in case they are missing out on something else, but they are very hard workers. Blessed with excellent ideas and creative streaks it can be a good idea for them to go into business for themselves. Sometimes selfish, they know what they want, often don't care if others want the same thing and can have a very nasty temper when pushed.

How to love a Sagittarian

Sagittarians love to travel and explore so let them be free and wild, and go to places they have never been before so they can broaden their horizons and experience new things. They don't like being cooped up in the home or stuck in the same situation for too long so allowing them to be versatile is crucial. Sagittarians are very honest and admire honesty in others so don't lie and keep things to yourself. Full of quirky ideas and a funny way of seeing the world, listen to their ramblings and enjoy the ride. A Sagittarian likes to be pushed to achieve. They admire ambition and love to achieve goals but they also love to see others achieve their goals too. They enjoy sex and like to try new things in bed to avoid becoming bored, so perhaps try some risky and unorthodox love making.

Capricorn

The Goat, 22nd December - 19th January

Element: Earth

Birthstone: Garnet

Tree: Birch

Planet: Saturn

Capricorns age well and often have lovely clear skin right into old age. Shy when you first meet them perhaps, they soon break out of their shell and can become one of the loudest people you will meet and also rather crude. Family orientated, they can be very moody, sometimes not even knowing why themselves. Indeed Capricorns do take life very seriously and crave security. But that's not to say they don't enjoy a good laugh because they do; they just don't have time for any silliness or stupidity. A Capricorn is usually very patient, which makes them brilliant workers, though often for the family and others more than themselves as they enjoy looking after people and being relied upon. Capricorns are also charming and can use their charm to get through any kind of problems.

How to love a Capricorn

Capricorns admire trustworthiness and stability; if you can give them that they will love you for it. Never be flaky or act dumb as a Capricorn doesn't find that an admirable quality. Indeed silly people annoy them. Help Capricorns relax because they feel pent up much of the time. Give them long sensuous massages and remember to look after them. Sometimes you may need to show them the lighter side of life. When it comes to sex, Capricorns can be rather aggressive and like energetic sex and being dominant.

Aquarius

The Water Bearer, 20ᵗʰ January – 18ᵗʰ February

Element: Air

Birthstone: Amethyst

Tree: Rowan

Planet: Uranus

Aquarians are fiercely independent and like to do everything their own way. If you tell them how to do something they simply will not listen most of the time and would rather make their own mistakes and learn on their own. You can usually tell an Aquarian because of the way they dress or the way they do things in a quirky way. Very intelligent, Aquarians are the thinkers of the zodiac, though they can be very bad time keepers because they do not go by time but instead their own pace and will not be rushed. Very friendly, they know lots of people and have many friends but also really appreciate their own company, enjoying sitting and thinking, trying to make sense of life and things that have happened. Aquarians are gentle people, friends of animals and the earth, and they'll fight for a cause or belief if they think there is injustice being done. In work, Aquarians are the big thinkers, not caring too much about small details but instead seeing the big picture. They can over think though and often find it hard to relax.

How to love an Aquarian

Aquarians love to give advice and it's usually good advice as they put a lot of thought into everything. Listen to their advice and they will really appreciate it. Debate with them; they love to talk about life and what it's all about. Let the Aquarian be independent too though; give them a sense of freedom because if they feel trapped they won't be around for long. Aquarians like long sensuous love making. They enjoy kissing and touching and are drawn to the meeting of minds as much as bodies.

Pisces

The Fishes, 19ᵗʰ February – 20ᵗʰ March

Element: Water

Birthstone: Aquamarine

Tree: Ash

Planet: Neptune

Pisceans can be intuitive and psychic, with an amazing ability to gage the world around them. Loving to learn about the metaphysical, whether spirituality or in the form of science and technology, they also want to know how things work and why people do the things they do. Another thing they love is talking and they can find it particularly hard to keep a secret because they don't like keeping things to themselves. They enjoy being on their own as well though, especially when carrying out creative projects or being creative with art, computers or something with tools. However, they can become depressed, moody or angry because their personality has so many different sides they sometimes don't know what they will be feeling from one moment to the next. Pisceans are particularly creative at work and will shrivel up and die in a dead end routine job; they need to be able to spread their creativity or they can become very unhappy.

How to love a Piscean

When Pisceans choose to love a person they often fall in deep, giving their whole heart. This can seem rather intense for some. Show Pisceans you're ready for this and that you want their love. Talk about emotions and how they make you feel. Start projects together and let them talk about their dreams and fantasies. Pisceans love to solve problems but don't let them take on too much; instead keep a certain amount of independence to keep the relationship healthy. Pisceans are erotic lovers, have a very playful personality and like fantasy and adventure, in the bedroom and outside of it.

"Trees are sanctuaries.
Whoever knows how to listen to them, can experience the truth.
They do not teach learning and precepts, they preach, undeterred by particulars,
the ancient law of life"

Herman Hesse

Celtic Tree Birth Signs

The Celts and Druids put a lot of faith in trees - to them the most sacred of things on earth. Of course this makes sense, given how important trees are. Not only are trees beautiful; they provide us with so many benefits, and these would have been much more welcome and necessary back in those days. Trees provided wood for home-building, fuel for cooking fires, for bringing light into darkness and warmth into cold, for keeping away wild animals. Trees produced fruit and nuts, sheltered birds, gave shade when the sun was scorching and generated oxygen. Their roots stretched down to the underworld and their branches reached up to the otherworld. This is shown in the Wiccan symbol of the Celtic tree, which has the trees bush on the top and the roots mirroring the bush. 'As above so is below.' We are also rooted in the earth and reaching upwards to the heavens.

The highly spiritual Celts understood that people bore a personality and likes or dislikes due to the period in which they were born. They attributed these characteristics towards their knowledge and love of trees. It is considered lucky to keep wood from your tree sign and many Wiccans fashion a wand made from a branch of their tree.

Below are the birth signs and meanings for each tree:

Birch

December 24th - January 20th

The birch sign is ambitious, a very good leader able to motivate and get others passionate about their ideas. The first tree to grow leaves after the winter months, the birch sign is a trend setter. Because you were born in a time of barren land and darkness you naturally seek light and warmth. Birches are tough and don't suffer fools gladly, putting great effort into getting things done and not letting others stand in their way. A birch loves light but also embraces darkness and is not afraid of their darker side.

The oil from birch bark is particularly healing for the skin and can also be used as an insect repellent. The bark itself can be used magically to ward off evil spirits and bad luck, and it will bring you courage and strength. Make a broom with birch and use it to sweep away negativity. Birch was the original yule log and was said to bring luck when burned on Yule night. The birch tree may look rather fragile, but it is one of the sturdiest trees there is, just like those born under its sign.

Rowan

January 21st - February 17th

Rowans are the intelligent sign within the tree zodiac. Full of creativity and ideas, they like to think things through and are sometimes misunderstood when they find it difficult to get their passion or ideas across to others. On occasions this leads to them shying away from getting to know people. They have a strong presence and people do not forget them in a hurry. The rowan sign are driven by their thoughts and ideas, which leads them to be very independent and wanting to do things their own way.

The growing of a rowan tree in a garden or near a home is said to attract the fae. Its berries are full of vitamin C and anti-toxins and make a lovely tea and you can keep bad luck away from you by tying a sachet of rowan berries with a white ribbon and hanging it in your kitchen. Rowan is also helpful with clearing the mind and opening our inspiration. Essence of rowan is used in vibrational medicine to assist in attuning us to nature, broadening perspectives, and for making room for a deeper understanding of our place here in the universe.

Ash

February 18th - March 17th

Druids saw the ash tree as enchanted and used its wood to make wands. People born under the time of the ash are usually interested in anything mystical, with a spiritual aspect to their personality. They enjoy being in nature and feel very much a part of it. This doesn't mean that those born under ash trees are flighty though; far from it. They keep their feet firmly on the ground and deal in reality, and often have a good understanding of science and how things work. Artistic too, enjoying crafts and working on their own, they can continue on a project non-stop if they are creating or making something new.

Ancient Greeks believed that humans were born from the ash tree and it was customary to plant one at the birth of a new baby, while in Norse belief the world of Yggdrasil was made from ash. And be warned! Ash trees attract lightning, so don't stand under one during an electric storm. But as for healing benefits, there are many. Its bark can make an infusion that is a mild laxative and diuretic. The root bark is the most potent with astringent properties, and was used to treat liver diseases and arthritic rheumatism. Other uses include reducing fever, treating kidney and urinary infections and expelling intestinal parasites. The leaves of the ash tree attract love and if you sleep with the leaves under your pillow they will bring on psychic dreams. Ash wood was used for the traditional handle of the besom broom and druid wands were often made of ash because of its straight grain, while the poles of witches' brooms were often made of ash and were representative of protection and strength. Ash wands are good for healing, and for general and solar magic.

171

Alder

March 18th - April 14th

Those born under the alder moon are confident to lead the way, with an excellent head for business. They can work their way up in a company because of their strong work ethic and because they are not afraid to take responsibility. With friends from all walks of life, their self-confidence is infectious and people enjoy being around them. Alders are doers and like to keep things moving, but sometimes struggle to find the right balance between work and play.

Alder was sacred to druids who made whistles from its wood. Its bark was used to treat skin inflammations, skin diseases and burns. A gift to the faerie world that allows access into their realm, alder is a wood of truth that brings things to the surface that were once hidden. When immersed in water it hardens to a toughness of stone, and when an alder grows its roots fertilise the soil and its timber resists decay. To summon help from the fae make a whistle of alder and call to them.

Willow

April 15th - May 12th

In Celtic belief the willow tree is associated with the moon. Those born under the willow are often highly intuitive and psychic, with a knack for knowing what will work and what won't. Willow signs can handle change excellently, just like the tree which grows fast and wildly. When life cuts them down they will quickly re-root and start again. And like the moon they are always going through cycles; their mood can change from hour to hour. Willow people have a light inside that is mysterious and many like to sit back in wonder and watch them glow. People born under the willow are often very beautiful; not in a conventional way but in a mysterious dark way.

Willow bark contains salacin, a main ingredient in aspirin, and so can be used as a pain killer. Made into a tea, it is particularly effective for arthritis, toothache and fevers. The sap from the willow is also excellent for treating skin conditions - especially acne. Willow is a tree of the moon and a sign of the divine feminine, the Goddess. Use it as a gift to the Goddess or as an offering. A beautiful and flexible wood for being creative with, witches brooms were traditionally bound with willow branches. It is a tree of the Sabbat Beltane. Stand under one on a full moon, blow the moon a kiss and make your wish.

Hawthorn

May 13th - June 9th

Those born under the hawthorn are like two different people, needing to keep a grounded and 'normal' life while inside they nurture dreams and passions that burn inside them. Hawthorn signs are excellent listeners and people will seek you out for advice, but you are also very good at talking and giving advice. Blessed with a creative streak that makes them excellent writers, photographers and artists, those born under the hawthorn moon can also be very spiritual. Hawthorn trees were sacred and planted in sacred places, such as churches, palaces and natural places of worship, as a means of protection.

The original maypoles of Beltane were made from the hawthorn tree. A great tree for protection, use its wood and thorns in appropriate magic. People made hedgerows of the hawthorn tree and its thorny barriers were used to keep unwanted people out of villages in ancient times. The flowers, leaves and fruits of the hawthorn have properties that reduce blood pressure and stimulate the heart, as well as acting as a mild sedative. In herbal medicine they can treat heart and circulatory disorders, migraine, menopausal conditions, angina, and insomnia. The flowers are strongest as sedatives, and can be used externally to treat acne and skin blemishes. The berries (also known as 'Pixie Pears') contain Vitamin B and Vitamin C. They can be crushed and used to ease diarrhoea, dysentery, and kidney disorders. However, it is strongly advised not to self-medicate with hawthorn because it can have a very powerful effect on the heart, which could be dangerous for those with hearts that are particularly weak.

Oak

June 10th - July 7th

People born under the great oak are truth seekers and protectors that can see badness and lies where others are unsure. It is difficult to put one over anyone born under the oak. In ancient times people made doors from oak believing it would keep evil out. And to the druids the oak was the most sacred of trees, their name descending directly from the word oak which in Celtic is 'duir.' An oak sign has great strength and courage and will usually be the first to stand up to bullies or anyone getting mistreated. Oaks also have a special affinity with the past and enjoy learning about anything historical.

The medicinal part of the oak is its bark, because of its strong astringent properties. As a tea it helps fight diarrhoea and dysentery. Externally it can be used to treat haemorrhoids, inflamed gums, wounds and eczema. The tannin found in oak can help reduce minor blistering by boiling a piece of the bark in a small amount of water until a strong solution is reached, and then applying to the affected area. To cure frostbite, American folk medicine called for collecting oak leaves that had remained on the tree all through the winter. These leaves were boiled to obtain a solution in which the frostbitten extremities would soak for an hour each day for a week.

It was said that dreaming of resting under an oak tree means you will have a long life and wealth, that climbing the tree in your dream means a relative will have a hard time of it in the near future, and that dreaming of a fallen oak symbolises loss of love. And that's not all; if you catch a falling oak leaf you shall have no colds all winter. If someone becomes sick, warm the house with an oak wood fire to shoo away the illness. Carry an acorn against illnesses and pains, for immortality and youthfulness, and to increase fertility and sexual potency. To aid fertility, bury the acorn on the ninth day.

Carrying any piece of the oak tree draws good luck to you, but always remember to ask permission and show gratitude. A protector and sacred to druids, King Arthur's round table was made from a single cross section of a large oak. On Litha make a fire with oak wood to bring luck for the year to come. And make an oak twig pentagram for protection.

Holly

July 8th - August 4th

Those born under the holly are of noble mindedness. Celts used to crown their high and noble leaders with a crown of holly. Confident, natural leaders, they refuse to let bad weather or hard times get them down, and are often at their best when times are dark. Able to lift spirits and very generous, holly people are also ambitious, competitive and intelligent, able to soak up information from all around. Holly trees are evergreen and fruit in the winter, and just like those born under their sign, nothing can shake them.

Associated with Yule, its red berries represent ovulation of the Goddess, while the white berries of mistletoe represent semen of the God. Holly is commonly used all over the world as a Christmas decoration, a custom derived from the early Romans who sent boughs of holly and other gifts to their friends during Saturnalia, the Roman festival of Saturn held around the 17th of December in celebration of the winter solstice. In pagan folklore the holly tree is associated with the spirit of vegetation and the waning forces of nature, personified as a mythical figure called the Holly King. The Holly King rules nature during its decline from the mid-summer solstice (Litha, Jun 21st) through to the mid-winter solstice (Yule, Dec 21st).

The Holly King is often depicted as an old man dressed in winter clothing, wearing a wreath of holly on his head and walking with the aid of a staff made from a holly branch. This is symbolic of the fertile interaction of the Goddess and God during natures decline and the darkest time of the year. At each of the solstice sabbats, the Holly King and his brother the Oak King engage in ritual combat for the attention of the Goddess, with the victor presiding over nature through the following half of the year.

As with many other trees the holly was revered for its protective qualities. When planted around the home it protects the inhabitants and guards against lightning, poisoning and mischievous spirits. Throwing a stick of holly at wild animals is said to make them leave you alone, while a piece of holly carried on your person is said to promote good luck, particularly in men - for the holly is a male plant, with the ivy being its female opposite. As a charm to enhance dreams, nine holly leaves gathered on a Friday after midnight, wrapped in a clean cloth to protect against its needles, and tied up using nine knots was placed under a pillow to make dreams come true. Some old stories tell us that when winter came the old druids advised people to take holly into their homes to shelter elves and fairies who could join mortals at this time without causing them harm. But these stories also tell of a warning; to remove holly entirely before the eve of Imbolc, for to leave just one leaf in the house would cause misfortune.

Holly leaves were formerly used as a diaphoretic and an infusion of them was given for catarrh, bronchitis, pneumonia, influenza, pleurisy and smallpox. They have also been used for intermittent fevers and rheumatism because of their tonic properties. The juice of the fresh leaves has been used to advantage in jaundice, and when sniffed was said to stop a runny nose. When soaked in vinegar and left for a day and a night, it was used to cure corns, and an old remedy for chilblains was to thrash them with a branch of holly to 'chase the chills out', but this could obviously be painful too.

The berries possess totally different qualities to the leaves, being violently emetic and purgative, and if swallowed can cause excessive vomiting. They have been used in dropsy, and in a powder form as an astringent to check bleeding. Nicholas Culpeper in 'The Complete Herbal', published in 1653, wrote "the bark and leaves are good used as fomentations for broken bones and such members as are out of joint". He also considered the berries to be curative of colic. Care needs to be taken however, for holly berries can be poisonous if given to children.

Hazel

August 5th - September 1st

Hazel is the most intelligent of the Celtic tree signs. With a thirst for knowledge and a great ability to retain it, hazel people are often good at reading people in an almost psychic way. To some the hazel sign might appear to be a bit of a know it all, but it is just their way, as they pick up things very quickly. Hazel signs like everything to be just right and are often seen as perfectionists. They make excellent leaders and teachers and like rules and structure, especially if it is their own rules and structure, but even though they are cool on the outside and don't seem to lack confidence, they are always seeking approval.

In Celtic folklore the hazel tree is considered a tree of knowledge, particularly in Ireland where its nuts are a symbol of great mystical wisdom. Hazel trees were also well known throughout Europe where they have been growing since prehistoric times, and where hazelnuts formed part of the staple food diet. An old custom was to use small flexible twigs from the hazel to secure grape vines to stakes. As the grape vine is sacred to Bacchus (the Roman god of intoxication and vegetation), any goats or other animals found feeding on the vines were caught and sacrificed to him on spits made of hazel.

Hazelnuts are rich in many vitamins and minerals, and are recommended to eat when you have any kind of digestive disorder. They are particularly rich in magnesium, a mineral the body needs to prevent heart disease, cancers and osteoporosis. Many people do not get enough magnesium in their diets but it is essential to us. Hazelnuts are very fatty but it is the good kind of fat called oleic acid, which is great for your organs and blood. One cup of hazelnuts contains 86% of the recommended daily allowance of vitamin E, and Vitamin E has been proven to protect skin from the harmful effects of ultraviolet radiation, such as skin cancer and premature aging.

Vine

September 2nd - September 29th

Vines are fast growing and ever changing, just like those born under this sign. They have an unusual amount of energy and people find it hard to keep up with them at times. There is a downside to this though, as they can end up exhausted and burnt out, and so they must learn to pace themselves. Vines love the luxuries in life and work very hard for them. They enjoy spending money on themselves and their loved ones and make excellent friends as they will do anything for someone they love. Because they can see both sides of everything, the good and the bad in every situation, they sometimes find it hard to make decisions.

Strictly not a tree, the vine is one of the oldest cultivated plants in the world and is sacred to Wiccans and druids alike. Vines produce grapes full of anti-toxins and vitamins and can be made into wine - and most of us know the effect that has on us! In fact the vine was a plant of Dionysus, the Greek God of wine. Ancient Egyptians meanwhile, made hieroglyphs and drawings of vine cultivating and wine making. Vines will grow anywhere and can grow up to fifteen metres in length and will often grow over anything that stands in their way. In magic, vines are used to give us energy. Keep branches from the vine and use it when going to job interviews or if you want to grow within yourself or spiritually.

Ivy

September 30th - October 27th

Ivy can also cling to anything and grow; it doesn't matter what you put in its way, it will simply keep going, just like those born under its sign. They will often shock people at how resilient they can be at overcoming any hurdles standing in their way. Blessed with a loyal nature, they are loving and giving when it comes to friends and family and are always on hand to help. Ivy signs are hard workers, stemming from their love of money and boundless energy. They enjoy talking and love a good gossip, but can feel the world is against them at times when they seem to be constantly struggling. However, this comes from them wanting to move on and get things done and their frustration that others do not move at the same pace.

Ivy is a scared plant, mostly associated with the holly tree. It attaches itself to almost anything and grows wildly, and is a representation of strength and determination. Never eat ivy or put it in your mouth as it is poisonous. Although very beautiful it also has a dark side and will envelop anything it touches, including other plants. In ancient times ivy was seen as a plant of artists and poets, with many wearing a crown of it on their heads. Throughout the ages it has also been seen as a sign of fidelity and fertility; in ancient times priests would put a garland of ivy around a groom. If you are trying to conceive, then place ivy on your altar.

Reed

October 28th - November 24th

Reeds were seen as trees to the Celts because of their deep roots - and those born under the sign do indeed have deep roots. Family means a great deal to them and their life revolves around the home. Unnaturally good at finding things out, they are the instinctive detectives of all the signs. Good secret keepers, especially about themselves, they may have hidden aspects about themselves under many layers. Honourable, they will never deceive you and will not appreciate anyone trying to deceive them. Do so at your peril as a reed has a temper that is unmatched by any other of the signs.

A reed is not a tree, but it is wooden, and in Scotland it is known as scotch broom. An all-round protector, it was one of the most scared shrubs used by the druids and represents Samhain (the Wiccan New Year). Symbolising renewal and cleansing, reeds make excellent wands and sceptres. People plant them on the edge of steep hills as their strong roots hold the earth together and stop the banks from toppling over. Reeds love to grow near water, making it a plant of the water element. When they grow along the sea and on cliffs they protect other species of plants from the harmful salty sea water sprays. And in ancient times reed was used to make parchment and paper and so is the plant of the Egyptian God Thoth. Associated with music, musical magic and calling the faerie world, Pan's flute is said to be made of reed.

Elder

November 25th - December 23rd

Those born under the elder are seekers, constantly looking for new adventure and opportunities. Elder people are often wild and do not like to be tamed, especially in their younger days. They will be at every party and nightclub going. When the elder sign matures though, their thoughts turn to travel and they want to explore the larger world. Natural money makers and money spenders they are rarely saving unless it's for travel or adventure. Elders are very spiritual and often contemplate the meaning of life and like to talk about the serious questions in life such as politics and religion. They also have an excellent sense of humour and can make people laugh easily.

Traditionally all parts of elder are useful medicinally; the berries and the leaves are both rich in vitamin C, with the berries particularly good for jam-making, or for wine, vinegar, and syrups; the leaves can be made into ear drops to treat pain and inflammation; the flowers make a tea that is good for treating coughs and irritable throats, as well as being made into a skin cleanser and lotion, while the bark of the new small twigs can be made into a laxative. Additionally, the bark, roots, berries and leaves can all be used as a dye.

The elder tree is wise and protective. It is like a father figure in our lives, so use it to ward off anything bad that befalls you. Keep the bark in your home to bring luck and to exorcise a space from harmful or bad energies. Use the berries to break spells cast against you. Put them in a bottle with some of your hair and nail clippings and a rusty nail and bury the bottle or jar outside your home - this will ward away any ill-intentioned spells.

"The Red Nation shall rise again and it shall be a blessing for a sick world;
a world filled with broken promises, selfishness and separations;
a world longing for light again.
I see a time of Seven Generations when all the colours of mankind
will gather under the Sacred Tree of Life
and the whole Earth will become one circle again.
In that day, there will be those among the Lakota
who will carry knowledge and understanding of unity
among all living things and the young white ones
will come to those of my people and ask for this wisdom.
I salute the light within your eyes where the whole Universe dwells.
For when you are at that centre within you
and I am that place within me, we shall be one"

Crazy Horse

Native American Animal Zodiac

Like the Druids of Ancient Britain, Native Americans placed a great deal of their spirituality into animals and animal totems. At one with nature and all within it, when someone was born they were given a totem animal, also called a solar totem, influenced by the relevant astrology. Native Americans would then grow and take on attributes of other animals or become fierce hunters, great cooks and good craftsmen. Their animal totem would therefore change over time, but they would always keep their birth animal and call upon them for guidance.

Below are the dates and personality traits of the Native American zodiac chart.

Otter

January 20th - February 18th

The otter is an individual, preferring to do things its own way. That's not to say it is the wrong way though, as their way is usually just as effective if not better than others. They like to think outside the box and tackle problems differently and intelligently. Brave and not caring what others think of them, otters dance to their own beat. Playful, with a wonderful sense of humour, they are kind and will fight for those they feel are getting a raw deal. Otters can go into themselves at times though, becoming lost in thought and, in extreme cases, isolated.

Wolf

February 19th - March 20th

The wolf is a lover and very independent. You cannot try and cage a wolf for it won't be around for much longer. Wolves need to be left to their own devices, to do what they need to do. This doesn't mean they are unfriendly; they love to be around people and will have a wide variety of friends from all walks of life. And they can be very intuitive, even psychic, with a knack for reading others. Wolves love crafting and working in balance with their hands and minds, and as we all know: a wolf can be a very fierce creature when cornered. So if you cross one, watch out; they do not suffer fools or conflict gladly.

Falcon

March 21st - April 19th

Falcons have a confidence most other signs do not have. This gives them excellent judgement and clear vision and makes them natural leaders, and because they can see things coming from a long way away and plan for any eventuality, falcons are always looking for opportunities. Then, when presented with them, they don't usually waste any time but instead jump straight in. They like to get things done and, to others, can come across as impatient and pushy. And there is some truth in that, as falcons can indeed be temperamental and easy to temper if things aren't going their way.

Beaver

April 20th - May 20th

Fantastic at adapting to change and making the best from any situation, beavers like to lead and be heard. Stalwarts that will work as hard as they need to get something done, they are not scared of hard work and have strength both inner and outer, with minds sharp and quick witted and bodies strong and enduring. A beaver can work on something repetitive for days on end if it means getting a task finished with a reward at the end. They like to make what they have grow; money, belongings, houses; they always want bigger and better and put everything into getting it.

Stag/Deer

May 21st - June 20th

The deer is one of the most intellectual of all Native American signs. Quick witted, they make excellent conversationalists and are brilliant at any kind of communication, whether it be verbal or written, because, most of the time, everything they say has been thought about deeply beforehand. Deer have a wonderful sense of humour and can make people laugh at will. They are changeable, though; one minute they can be on top of the world but the next they can be feeling rather depressed. This is because their minds are always ticking away and as one thought changes to another in an instant, so does their moods.

Woodpecker

June 21st - July 21st

Woodpeckers can be mysterious and keep much to themselves. Their lives revolve around their home and they need a safe and comfortable base in which to go to for rest and relaxation after a busy day. They have two sides to their personalities; one a confident and devil may care attitude that they show to most people, and the other a caring softer more sensitive side they keep for those very close to them. Woodpeckers love money and are excellent savers, never spending when they do not need to. Much of the money they do spend will be on making their home and personal environment as comfortable and secure as possible. With a belief in romance and love, woodpeckers mate for life.

Salmon

July 22nd - August 21st

Salmon are positive and energetic and find it hard to sit still or be stuck in a situation for too long. Filled with boundless energy and enthusiasm they need to keep moving and keep things fresh and new or they can become bored rather very quickly. Salmon usually have lots of friends and people love them because of their free spirit and energy levels. They also have a remarkable and sharp sense of humour, which can sometimes be at the expense of others. Ambitious and competitive, they love a good challenge, both physically and intellectually.

Bear

August 27th - September 21st

Bears are methodical and level headed and you can rely on them to help you out as they are very caring and often work in a sector that needs this characteristic. Clean and with a necessity for neatness that comes from needing to keep things in order within their own heads to be able to function to their fullest, bears can also tend to be a little shy. They do not see the point in making a big show of themselves, but instead let their work and inner self-confidence do the talking. The most patient of all Native American signs, they have an unshakeable belief that what they want will come to them through hard work and subtle motions. Bears are strong and not easily scared but brave beyond doubt.

Eagle

September 22nd - October 22nd

Eagles are majestic and have a natural charm that ensures people warm to them immediately. They can be looked upon as the settler of arguments because they respect others views and always keep a sense of fairness. Eagles like to spend money on themselves and on loved ones and find it hard to save as they live in the moment, but often they are still very good at handling money and making it last. And as eagles are famed for their sight and accuracy, people born under their sign can often spot anything wrong in a situation straight away and know how to put it right. An excellent ally to have on your side!

Snake

October 23rd - November 22nd

Snakes are secretive and only show you what they want you to see. But you can't hide anything from a snake; they are like detectives in their ability to wriggle out secrets from others. Spiritual and mysterious with a clear thought in their belief system, snakes like to be correct and, if made a fool of, can quickly turn nasty. They do love to laugh though, and can find humour in most things. And with their deep emotional nature they put everything into whatever they are doing, whether work, play or relationship. Natural winners, very good at games and sport with their competitive edge, when a snake wants something it rarely lets anything stand in its way.

Owl

November 21st - December 21st

The owl is a lover of life, absorbing masses of information and wanting to experience all that life has to offer. Philosophers, they like to question everything and learn others views and opinions on things and they love a good debate on issues of the day. Owls love to travel and be outdoors and they love the night. They work hard and party harder and on the outside seem like fun loving happy go lucky types, but deep down they have an unquenchable thirst for knowledge on the big questions of life, such as religion, politics and the afterlife.

Goose

December 22nd - January 19th

The goose is a hard worker that will set themselves a goal and stick to it until it is finished. With an internal voice that does not let them give up on things, the goose is very practical and lives in the real world, not appreciating fancy thrills and pomp but instead preferring things and people who are down to earth. They do need to watch their pessimistic side though, as they can tend to draw on negatives rather than positives in life. Very ambitious and high achievers once they set themselves great targets, goose are extremely loyal and will be first on the scene if one of their friends is in trouble.

Some Final Thoughts

There has been a massive shift in human consciousness lately. People in their thousands have been taking to the streets and protesting about injustice and unfairness, about huge conglomerates poisoning food and water in the name of profit. People are becoming tired of having lies spoon-fed to them and are becoming increasingly aware they are being controlled for the profit of the few. Many of us are fed up with the path society is forcing upon us and are reverting to nature to find our own balance and that of the world. We are taking back control of what we eat, watch, wear and listen to, and of what we understand and come to know.

In Wicca we learn to become one with nature, we learn balance within ourselves and with our surroundings, and we learn how to use the power of nature, of the earth and the elements, in order to heal and empower ourselves.

The Goddess gave birth to the universe which means she is in everything, from the smallest grain of grass to the biggest star. Her divine power is in all of us too, something which western science has finally caught up with, through its 'discovery' of what they call DNA, the instruction code for every living organism. Celebrate the fact we are all connected through the Goddess. Almost all early civilizations, with the vast majority of these having no contact with each other, knew that the Goddess was the creator of all. It has only been in the last few thousand years that the monotheistic religions have suppressed the Goddess in favour of a single male God figure.

Wicca is about believing in magic, believing in a connectedness to all things through the Goddess. It is about believing in yourself and believing you have the power to change things as you learn from the natural world. It is about creating harmony with everything around you so that you can bring about an inner peace. How you choose to do this is your own individual spiritual path and no one has the right to tell you if it is right or wrong.

Anyone can be Wiccan if this is the path they have chosen. You do not have to be in a coven or group and you do not have to be initiated by anyone to become Wiccan. Once you have chosen this path as your faith then, my friend, you are indeed Wiccan. And people find Wicca in many different ways, but it doesn't matter why or how you got here; what matters is that you

have now decided this feels right for you, or that someone else is showing you a sign by giving you this book as a present. Don't let anyone tell you that you are wrong for being Wiccan or that it is evil or bad because it is not; it is simply natural. Ignore such people, or even better, educate them. People can be afraid of something that is unknown to them or something they don't understand, and it is not their fault that monotheistic religions and society have blinkered our connection to nature, to the universe and the Goddess. The only thing many know about Wicca is what they have heard from newspapers or ill-informed stories, or from Hollywood movies wishing to sensationalise.

Wicca is a recognised religion and you have the freedom of practicing your religion just as much as a devotee of any other religion. Slowly but surely, this freedom is being granted around the world. Sabbat festivals are bigger than ever now, with record numbers visiting Stonehenge on the Solstices, and with Sabbat festivals being hosted by many major cities. People all over the world are returning to their connection with the beauty and harmony of nature. More and more are turning to natural and herbal remedies for sickness, are growing their own fruit and vegetables and taking notice of the seasons and harvests. The world is turning full circle. More and more people are reverting to paganism and Wicca, making it one of the fastest growing religions in the world today. There are thousands of Wiccan groups and Covens sprouting everywhere and record numbers of people choosing handfasting ceremonies over 'traditional' weddings. American, Canadian, Australian and many other countries military organisations now recognise Wicca as a religion and will allow a full military burial with the pentagram put on grave stones as a religious symbol. Wicca can be put on military dog tags too and there are many Pagan and military groups to support Wiccan soldiers and their families. We are returning to what we once knew and took for granted.

Wiccans come in every shape, sexuality, colour and class. Wiccans are me and they are you. We come from all walks of life, from every part of the world. Be proud to call yourself pagan. Be proud to call yourself Wiccan. It may be a cliché but it's true; together, we can make a huge difference.

Thank you for reading and Blessed Be.

Printed in Great Britain
by Amazon.co.uk, Ltd.,
Marston Gate.